IS IT BEAUTIFUL?

A Journey from Separation toward Unification

Betty A. Luceigh, PhD

BALBOA.
PRESS
A DIVISION OF HAY HOUSE

Balboa Press books may be ordered through booksellers or by contacting:

Balboa Press
A Division of Hay House
1663 Liberty Drive
Bloomington, IN 47403
www.balboapress.com
1 (877) 407-4847

Because of the dynamic nature of the Internet, any web addresses or
links contained in this book may have changed since publication and may
no longer be valid. The views expressed in this work are solely those
of the author and do not necessarily reflect the views of the publisher,
and the publisher hereby disclaims any responsibility for them.

The author of this book does not dispense medical advice or prescribe the
use of any technique as a form of treatment for physical, emotional, or medical
problems without the advice of a physician, either directly or indirectly. The
intent of the author is only to offer information of a general nature to help you
in your quest for emotional and spiritual well-being. In the event you use any
of the information in this book for yourself, which is your constitutional right,
the author and the publisher assume no responsibility for your actions.

Any people depicted in stock imagery provided by Thinkstock are models,
and such images are being used for illustrative purposes only.
Certain stock imagery © Thinkstock.

Print information available on the last page.

ISBN: 978-1-5043-8422-3 (sc)
ISBN: 978-1-5043-8421-6 (hc)
ISBN: 978-1-5043-8423-0 (e)

Library of Congress Control Number: 2017948046

Balboa Press rev. date: 08/04/2017

DEDICATION

*To the future that is never present until it arrives
and to Beauty that is ever present on the way.*

ACKNOWLEDGMENTS

I gratefully acknowledge the many who have inspired and influenced my life. I thank those who have been especially supportive as I wrote this book: Cynthia Pearson, Jann McGuire and participants of her spiritual group, participants of my Brain Group, and Fran Wheatley. I thank readers for their insightful feedback: Olive Riley, Jann McGuire, Marie Soleil, Louise Jackson, Robert Goings, and Bill Haxton. I thank the abundance of teachers in my life, including my students, parents, brother, and sister. I thank the authors of the many books I have read over the years on science and on spirituality. I acknowledge recent authors who continue to have a deep impact on me: Ken Wilber (for his keen integrative intellect), Adyashanti (for his clear and inspiring expressions of the heart), and Richard Rohr (for his healing insights into the Christian tradition). I thank my dog Ribo for his constant smile and companionship. Finally and most significantly, I thank Mother Nature for giving us life that allows these experiences to happen among us on beloved Earth.

PREFACE

This book is about my personal relationship with Beauty—not beauty as in the familiar meaning of glamor or elegance but Beauty in the spiritual context of an Absolute Essence. This is my story before and after my direct experiential encounter with Beauty's presence as all-encompassing radiance. Before that experience, my life was separated into two pathways: science and spirit. After Beauty's gift, those pathways moved toward unification as I expanded my awareness of being human.

I have organized this book into several parts: the first is autobiographical to provide some of the major events of my life as context; the second is to illustrate, through several poems and reflections, the way in which I now contemplate life and its meaning; and the last is to reveal in more depth the nature of my current spiritual journey as an elder.

My life is a sample of many aspects of the times from 1943 to the present and hence illustrates some of the broader changes occurring in my seventy-three-year period of history. I serve as one example of women in a profession once limited to men, the science of chemistry. I reveal my dilemmas, torn between a path of science and a path of spirit, which seemed incompatible. I share how my expanding heart as an adult sought spiritual liberation from the religious limitations of my strict Catholic upbringing. I represent some of the difficulties of marital relationships as society began to redefine a woman's role and marriage. I also demonstrate the impact of transitioning from communication devices before the 1980s to rapidly expanding new technologies since.

My deepest needs have always been for creative expression and spiritual reflection. Blessed with a diversity of beloved friends, I find my most intimate spiritual connection to Beauty which embraces us all.

As I wrote about my life at different stages, I found my mode of expression often reflected my level of awareness at the corresponding time. Thus, you may sense within the writing an arc of several developmental progressions along the way. I have interspersed some of my poems written during the time of described events; they also change in style and content over the years.

I purposely limited usage of certain words, such as *god* and *love,* as these often have multiple interpretations unrelated to my intent. I prefer words such as *Divine, Oneness, Essence,* or *Wholeness* which I will capitalize to indicate an all-inclusive principle. I consider myself "spiritual but not religious," in the sense that I don't belong to any one organized religion but rather integrate my own reflections and experiences with spiritual wisdom from many others.

I wrote this book to honor and share Beauty's role in my life. I encourage others to share what they value most in theirs. I believe a better future for all humanity begins with each of us becoming our very best individual human being. If each of us strives toward our highest potential with integrity and kindness, all of us will ultimately benefit. It has taken courage to write this book, but I believe I must leave any gift I may have for others in gratitude for the many who have left theirs for me.

For Beauty's sake,
Betty Luceigh

CONTENTS

INTRODUCTION

Separation and Unification
Hold hands
Dance
Every where
Every now.

To say I began life as the unification of one human egg cell and a sperm is a convenient event for reference. Yet it is somehow incomplete, for the story of my own life has unfolded and will continue to unfold in relation to everything gone before me and everything happening now. My initial physical constituents, from atoms to cells, were created long before I was. This occurred during the evolution of the Universe from the Big Bang through life on Earth. To be aware of the deep complexity of universal matter and energy within which my life now exists is to experience it within a context of expanded meaning. It is a meaning embracing the recurring processes of separation and unification over space and time.

The fertilization of a human egg is itself an event of unification. However, separation quickly follows. The first cell divides into two and those into more and more. Based on DNA-directed differentiation in their characteristics and functions, cells further separate from other cells. Those with shared features unite into regional collections to become organs, bones, circulatory systems, and all other building blocks of a human body. Separate but interactive, they unify to define a living being.

The overwhelmingly intricate initial phase of human development occurs with the fetus dependent on its placental connection to the mother's womb. Then a dramatic separation of the baby from that womb occurs. We celebrate the physical disconnection as birth and mark the time and place. My celebration occurred November 11, 1943, in Dallas, Texas.

Separations and connections continue after birth during stages of human development based on both genetic and environmental factors. For example, expressions of behavioral development may occur as social interactions. As a very young child, I separated the *me* inside my body from the *you* outside. As a teenager, I connected to others of my age and interests while separating *us* from *them.*

The overlapping of all separations and connections along all developmental lines—such as physical, intellectual, emotional, social, and moral—creates a complex interwoven pattern of evolving human details seemingly impossible to disentangle. Ultimately, the inherent human objective appears to be to sustain one's body with interconnected internal and external systems working cooperatively for the expression of the highest potential, however defined, of the whole human.

The activities of separation and unification, most of which occur unconsciously, are essential for the expression and continuation of life. This is a mystery in itself. However, the even greater mystery is how all these different processes are occurring while we have the conscious experience of being a single entity we call a *self*. I know myself as the same person of my youth and simultaneously know I am not the same. I seem to be my own paradox of constancy and change.

I believe changes within me when I was about six years old marked the beginning of a major conscious separation in my understanding of being the human, Betty. It was more than thirty years later before that understanding deeply shifted toward unification. That shift has brought me now, more than another thirty years later, to focus on the question, "Is it Beautiful?"

PART I

AUTOBIOGRAPHY

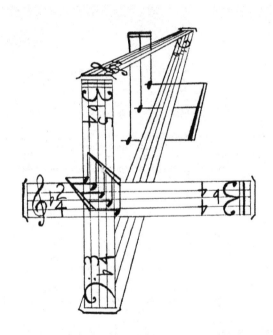

See Clef

Pencil Drawing, Luceigh 1979

SEPARATION BEGINS

Child
Questions
Synaptic abundance
"Why" births Y
Discernment divides
Longing begins
Return me.

Background

S ome early memories of my parents when we lived in Dallas, Texas, come easily and are indicative of the times (1943-1952).

Dad worked as an electrical engineer for the petroleum industry inventing ways to find oil. He would go on trips to search for new oil sites. I remember giving him a big hug to welcome him home from such a trip, but I had mumps at the time and knew nothing of transmittable diseases. I learned by the next day or so what those big words meant when I saw that Dad's puffy face looked like mine. I remember riding on Dad's shoulders during a Texas-size lightning-and-thunder storm. I held on tightly as he took me to the garage with the big door open so I could safely watch and listen to the storm and overcome my fear. I remember watching in horror as he beheaded the chickens we raised for dinner. Mostly, I remember his workshop, where he spent many hours doing strange things with strange tools on strange-looking devices.

Mother was a housewife with three children. She de-feathered and cooked those headless chickens, taught me the dangers of putting a knife in the toaster to get out the stuck toast, and let me lick chocolate chip cookie dough off the beater blades. I would help her hang the washed clothes out on the drying line or find the hamster when it got out of its cage. Mostly, I remember her keeping my school uniforms cleaned and pressed, driving me to the Catholic school, making my first communion dress, and helping me practice my catechism lessons.

I believe I was around six years old when I had two events that changed my awareness about the world: I became aware of human creativity from a television set, and I became aware of infinity from my catechism.

Betty as Angel, Age 6

The Television-Set Awakening

I had been taught that "in the beginning" (of what, I wasn't sure), God created everything. I had taken it very literally. I thought I was in school to learn what was already created. In fact, that was true in the beginning of my education, when the school focus was on reading, writing, arithmetic, and recess—although I doubt I believed God had created the latter.

One day in the late 1940s, I walked into Dad's workshop and saw a wooden box with an eight-inch square cut out of the front. Something glass filled the hole. Most of the time, the front glass had an image of circles, lines, and an Indian head. Dad spent hours either adjusting knobs to make the image very clear or working with his hands inside the back of the box. He seemed to be having fun, but I thought it was boring and preferred to spend my time hunting for tadpoles and turtles at a nearby creek. Then one day, I passed by the front glass in the box and saw a man walking in a funny way making funny faces while music played along. It turned out to be Charlie Chaplin.

It was then that I asked Dad, "What *is* this box?"

He told me, "It's a television set, a TV. We will be able to see pictures and hear sounds from it, sometimes from places far away from home. Many people worked many years to invent it. This is one of the first ones available to buy."

I left his workshop very puzzled because I thought all things were already created. How could there be this brand-new thing? Surely God hadn't just made it and put it here! Dad said humans had created it over years. I thought, *If humans can create TVs, then they can create other things. Humans could invent new devices!* I may have looked around the house and realized the toaster and electric beater in the kitchen were in the same category: invented! I wondered if this was what Dad had been doing in his workshop all this time. I reasoned that if things could be invented or created by humans, then I myself could become an inventor or creator of new things when I grew up. There could be many new things in the world in the future. My imagination had a curtain of misinformation ripped away! I was very excited!

The Catechism Awakening

One time, I started to think about what "forever and ever" really meant. It appeared frequently in catechism answers and at the end of almost all prayers. I thought, *Just how long is that, anyway?* I lay on my bed, shut my eyes, and tried to imagine myself in heaven, a place where "forever and ever" occurred. What would it be like? I assumed there were still days and nights, and I had been told about angels, clouds, and singing, but not much more.

I imagined that on the first day, I would sing songs with the angels; the next day, I would jump from cloud to cloud; the third day, I would dance around with an angel; the fourth day, I would listen to a harp; and so it went. Then I ran out of ideas of what to do, so I had to imagine repeating these entertainments, and repeating, and repeating, and repeating. It finally struck me that "forever and ever" really meant it would go on and on and on! It would never stop— never! I didn't know the word *infinity* at that time, but the concept was there. My child brain couldn't process this concept, and I got very scared, jumped out of bed, and ran to Mother. I told her, "I was trying to figure out 'forever and ever,' but I can't do it, and I'm scared." I don't remember what specifically she said, but she let me snuggle up to her and diverted my attention by talking of other finite things.

I thought it best if I never again tried to figure out how long "forever and ever" was. I had never experienced an idea that my mind could not at all grasp. It seemed to send my mind into a whirl. Perhaps I feared the whirling would continue "forever and ever."

Initial Separation

These two childhood experiences represented new ways of thinking and approaching my world at an early age. I view them in retrospect as an introduction to two paths of knowledge. They illustrate the beginning of my internal separation into two contrasting activities: one related to creative thinking, the other to spiritual beliefs. When I was a child, my understanding was very simple. No doubt I noticed their primary events occurred in different locations: school or church. For one, I sat at a desk; for the other, I knelt. I might have used words such as *learning* and *praying* instead of *science* and *religion*. I doubt I was aware that each used different methods of gathering and processing information. Everything indicated that these paths were to be kept separate in life. There appeared to be some kind of rule about this somewhere, and I accepted it as truth from the adults.

I had to get much older before I wondered whether creativity itself might go on forever and ever. It may have been about the time I also questioned whether the rule of separation was false.

Chapter 2

LIVING TWO PATHWAYS: PHASE ONE

1952-1983

Learning
Living
One travels as two
Identity expands space
Stability plays hide-and-seek
Sip of liberation.

Grade School

At some point in my early education, I had been told how fortunate I was because I was born in the greatest state in the United States (Texas) and the greatest country in the world (the United States) and the one true religion (Catholicism). I always thought this was very odd. I wondered why I would be so lucky and what would happen to all those other people who were not Texan, American, *and* Catholic.

However, I became less fortunate by these criteria

when our family moved to Tulsa, Oklahoma, after I completed fourth grade.

I went to Catholic schools from first through eighth grade, so it was natural that the path of religion had a very strong presence during those years. Almost anything we did at school had religious doctrine built into or around it. I truly enjoyed learning. Both reading and math became more and more interesting as each year passed. I was happy to go to the chalkboard and solve a multiplication problem or stand up from my desk—after raising my hand, of course—to spell a polysyllabic word. During this time, I had my first inkling that I might become a teacher when I grew up. One thing I knew for sure was that I would *never* hit the hand of every student in the class with a ruler just because one student wouldn't admit to breaking a rule.

In sixth grade, a nun started teaching me to play the piano. I practiced on an old upright stored in a junk-filled, dusty room at school. I loved that room! I was left alone to practice the piano while others went out to recess. Connecting the musical symbols to finger movements that made sounds was an all-absorbing activity. That storage room became a refuge where I could freely practice self-expression in a new way. Eventually, my parents brought a spinet piano home. The sound was better, but I was never sure why the sense of refuge was not quite the same.

I have wondered about my experience first learning to express music by playing the piano. It had a profound impact on me, but then, I was a preteen and everything was intensified. Music was an intellectual challenge, involved physical coordination, and evoked new emotions. Something about music seeded in me a sense of connection, maybe like a wire Dad would solder between two electrical components in his TV. Certainly it connected my touch on an invented device to a sound that traveled forever and ever. I wonder now if my time in that dusty storage room was actually a refuge from maintaining the hidden conflict of my internal separation.

High School

You might imagine my protestations and tears when my parents sent me to a *public* high school. How could I be in a place without religion interwoven into everything? Would I have to keep my "only true" religion a secret? How could I make the sign of the cross before an exam with non-Catholics watching?

Although I maintained my devotion to Catholicism, my concerns about public school surprisingly underwent conversion. It was a new reality. The high school, Thomas A. Edison in Tulsa, was educationally excellent. I learned how to write original works, took Latin as my first foreign language, studied math through calculus, had two years of chemistry, and excelled in all of them. My senior science project won me local and statewide awards. My perfect score on the math Scholastic Aptitude Test (SAT) shocked even me. I continued piano lessons from a Tulsa University instructor. I never learned to relax playing recitals. It just wasn't the same as drawing numbers on the chalkboard.

Along the way, I made friends with people who practiced different religions but valued similar intellectual interests. My measure of a *shocking* event was when I smelled cigarette smoke coming from a bathroom stall. What I was clueless about, and just assumed was another adult rule, was why all the students in my high school were white. During these years, I expanded socially, blossomed intellectually, developed my teenage identity, began to date, had my first kiss, and dreamed of my life goals. Many times in my life, I have thought about how fortunate I was to have those opportunities. I was appalled when I discovered years later that not all high schools were like mine and not all children had the same options. It was another example of separation that made no sense to me.

My high school experiences reinforced my view that I could have a pathway of science and a pathway of religion if I just kept them separate. There was a kind of logic about it. Science clearly did not include any part of religion, and religion simply ignored science as having any value. Science had nothing to do with the soul, and religion had nothing to do with rational, objective, critical thinking.

Music I left unclassified. When I played the piano, sometimes I sensed the order and creative expression I associated with science, and sometimes I sensed the emotions I associated with spirit. By then, however, I was a full-blown teenager who also loved to rock 'n' roll the night away at dances in the gym. Sometimes, it was just more fun to sweat in my loafers than reflect on anything.

I had my first crush on the teacher of an English class, and this helped motivate me to expand my vocabulary. My *Roget's College Thesaurus* was one of my sacred books until the teacher told me one of my essays was *sesquipedalian*. How embarrassing! I discovered writing poetry and loved playing with words and metaphors. The first poem I recall writing during my senior year in high school (1960-1961) was about chemistry and love (think *teenager*). It was titled "The Atomic Theory of Love." I felt I was breaking the rules about separating science and religion but decided that maybe poetry, like music, was unclassified in my separation scheme. I mark that experience as a sign, probably unconscious, that I wanted to combine them. Perhaps the separation was beginning to feel more like a conflict.

I believe this subdued sense of conflict showed up later within the same year when I wrote a poem called "Stuck." It began:

> I have one world in my head,
> Another in my belly.
> I am stuck in the butter
> Between the bread and jelly.
>
> One is a world of reason,
> The other of mystery.
> My feet take turns along the shore
> Between the sand and sea.
> ...

It goes on to explore this theme and ends with what became a profound challenge to myself.

> ...
> I am stuck between these worlds
> And all I want to know
> Is how it's possible to have them both
> And not let either one go.

Travels

After high school, while I was working toward my undergraduate degree, I had my first trip out of the United States. I spent the summer of 1962 in Guatemala as a volunteer for the Maryknoll missionaries. Side trips took me to see populated Maya villages and very remote sites that exposed me to extreme native poverty. Through it all, I observed exceptional acts of kindness and charity by the Maryknolls. This first direct experience in another culture expanded my awareness of other human beings far beyond Texans and Oklahomans.

What I cannot imagine now is why I was not yet aware that similar situations also existed within the United States. I still find it inexplicable that in high school I learned nothing detailed about the African American community across the Arkansas River in Tulsa, nor anything other than a few stereotypes about the Native American tribes in Oklahoma. I have wondered in my later years why, in 1962, I knew more about the lives of non-whites in a foreign country than those right in my own local area in America. It was a long time before I realized that silence about something difficult could be a way to deny it exists at all.

My second trip out of the United States was to Japan in 1966, just before beginning graduate school. My first husband, a navy pilot during the Vietnam War, was stationed five months at the base in Iwakuni. Living there with him, I had many wonderful opportunities to experience the Japanese landscape and culture. One experience, however, was not so wonderful.

We lived near Hiroshima, and my trip alone to the museum and ground zero of the nuclear bombing of 1945 deeply awakened me to the horrors of nuclear war. It had only happened twenty-one years earlier, two years after my birth. My memory of the museum, especially the human form burned into concrete steps, is vivid to this day. I had a difficult time realizing *my* country had dropped that horrific bomb, even though I knew of the Pearl Harbor attack that had brought the United States into the war. Remembering my first awareness that war means suffering on *both* sides still brings me to tears. Nonetheless, while stationed there, I was always treated kindly by the Japanese people I met. In return, I gave many eager strangers a chance to practice speaking English.

During our time in Japan, my husband and I made one side trip to Hong Kong, long before its return to the Chinese. The closest I got to China was to look at it behind a border fence while on a bus tour. Hong Kong in 1966 exposed me to a startling contrast between abject poverty and extravagant wealth. I could not grasp the extremes of living conditions in such close proximity. Other than the flashing neon signs, it is not the elegant structures I remember. It is the cardboard or metal shelters of the poor on the side of a steep, muddy hill, as well as families housed in simple boats on the putrid waters.

These were not my only trips out of the United States, but they happened when I was a naive young adult. I never forgot what I saw and felt during those experiences. I am grateful for the beautiful places I visited, but especially for the difficult lessons about living conditions of people in other parts of the world.

Between these travels, I took a different kind of trip within the United States, a trip of shock and grief. In 1963,

President John F. Kennedy was assassinated. At twenty years old, I simply couldn't comprehend such a thing happening within my own country and, like many others at that time, I still remember events in fine detail. I was bringing in groceries to the kitchen of our apartment, and I put the brown paper bag on the countertop, with the fridge to the left and a sunlit window and small table with my manual typewriter to the right. I turned on a portable radio as it was reporting the news, and I stood there frozen. It helps me now understand why I so often heard about the Great Depression but never had the emotional response of those who actually lived through it. I learned a lesson about how a real *experience* is very different from a *description* of an event.

University

Between the ages of seventeen and twenty-six, my higher education focused on science. I chose chemistry as a major for my BS (University of California, Berkeley, 1966) and organic chemistry for my PhD (Stanford University, 1970). I fell in love with organic chemistry when I took my first course as an undergraduate. I was excited by the art of drawing organic chemical structures, what they represented in real life—both biological and non-biological—and the logic of reaction processes. It was very clear to me that my passion for science and specifically teaching organic chemistry was my professional calling. Along the way, however, *life* happened, and many situations got complicated.

During that time period (1963-1970), I lived primarily in California, married *and* divorced my first husband, left the

Catholic religion, and was ostracized by my family. The Vietnam War was in progress, and the hippie generation was blooming.

I thrived during all my chemistry education, even though the schedule was very demanding. The foundation for my professional pathway of scientific knowledge in organic chemistry was strongly established. I released Catholicism gradually until I made the final decision that I no longer felt honest claiming I was a Catholic. I experienced a genuine liberation from the rituals and dogmas but stayed connected to my inner spiritual life. I began my own spiritual search by reading books, attending events where I sat on the floor, writing new poetry, playing piano—all without using any drugs! I still held the two big pathways, science and spirit, separate, but with less internal conflict and more curiosity. I also had some fun along the way, as exemplified in the following poem, though written years later, about atoms in humans.

Sitting with Atoms
(c. 2005)

Who would sit together with me,
human with human, in uncertainty,
aware of my atoms sitting with yours,
as yours with mine, to be sure,
knowing without atoms there would be
no experience at all sitting as we,
for unless our atoms connect to shape life,
we'll have no memory what sitting was like.

Atoms needed humans to identify them
and we need atoms to comprehend

both atoms into humans, then atoms back
recycling matter into a new pack.
So sit with me now to treasure what's borrowed,
uncertain of whether we'll sit so tomorrow,
but certain our atoms will quickly forget
the memory of us when they disconnect.

Leaving Chemistry

My life as a woman in chemistry had its own difficulties. As long as I was a busy student fulfilling degree requirements, I didn't pay much attention to the subtle signs of prejudice. As soon as I started to look for a job in the 1970s, the reality hit hard. I had remarried and had some limitations due to my husband's work location, but I just kept moving forward professionally as best I could. I did postdoctoral chemical research for several years and then began to teach organic chemistry at the university level at Santa Clara University in California. I was thrilled to be teaching chemistry at last!

Along the way, I sometimes turned to another form of self-expression: amateur artwork. I painted the acrylic piece below while in a whimsical mood. The original is in color, but within the black-and-white photo, one can still find musical notations, parts of a piano, and other elements of music. Whenever I hadn't looked at it for a long time, I often made a game of identifying all the symbols I had interwoven. One hand from the piano is playing the player's brain while the other picks a note. Such fun! Later I came to look at this work as a visual statement that *everything is connected through music.*

Music Composition, 1972

When my second husband accepted a tenured position in 1975, we moved from California to Cleveland, Ohio. During that time (1975-1978), not only did Mother die after years of cancer, but I felt almost ostracized again—this time as a woman in chemistry. It was fine for me to do research as long as it was in my *husband's* lab. The department chairman of chemistry *let* me teach organic chemistry because of an elderly instructor's sudden illness, but it was my enthusiastic students who made sure I *kept* teaching.

Since my chemistry position was part-time, I enrolled simultaneously as a student in the university's music department. It had a joint program with the Cleveland Institute of Music. I was challenged by an exceptional piano teacher and had my first experience taking music theory classes. I loved teaching my organic chemistry students, and I loved my piano lessons and music courses. I kept these two major activities separate, with one notable exception. I accompanied one of my organic chemistry students for an oboe piece he played for his music recital final exam. I was delighted when he passed both his oboe recital *and* organic chemistry!

Toward the end of the 1970s, I felt completely defeated in chemistry. It was not because of the students or my ability to teach, as I had excellent rapport and reviews. It was because of the way the chemistry profession treated women—sometimes subtle, sometimes blatant. The breaking point occurred when I was asked to give a presentation at a local women's college, not because of the quality of, or interest in, my research or teaching. It was to show them I could do chemistry *just like a man.* I made a deeply painful decision to discontinue all chemistry while I reevaluated my goals.

My husband and I returned to California because of his work, and I continued my music studies at the University of Southern California in Los Angeles. For a year, all was going well, and I was happy again. It was temporary. I was abruptly devastated by an unexpected divorce. It forced me to give up being a music student in order to seek employment. Holding back tears as I tried to appear confident during interviews was horrible. I first found an administrative position in the music department where I had been studying; then I moved into another administrative position in the chemistry division at the California Institute of Technology (Caltech) in Pasadena.

Some of the difficulties of the later 1970s I expressed in poems. I used writing to ease the suffering. This example is about divorce.

Dry Rain
(1979)

The tears flow silently from my heart
to rain upon my spirit
and leave my eyes dry to gaze
as empty of tears
as of the sight of you.

An inner cacophony began among my roles: musician, chemist, student, teacher, administrator, poet, relationship partner, renter, homeowner, spirit explorer, life explorer, mid-to-late-thirties single woman. Yikes! This uproar of identities makes it sound like a crazed time, but it wasn't—well, not entirely. Somehow, I found the courage and resilience to face all of it as it evolved. I did cry frequently and was overly stressed, but I just kept going until I finally found some stability. By thirty-nine, I was a first-time homeowner, working as a chemistry division head administrator, dating, occasionally teaching evening classes in chemistry, writing poetry, and playing piano. Formalized religion was not part of my life, but I continued to explore and treasure my spirituality through books and reflections. However, my spiritual life frequently took second place to keeping up with day-to-day responsibilities.

Then an experience spontaneously happened in 1983 that defied everything I ever thought I knew about anything. Prior to that, I had written the poem below, "Abyss." It expresses what I was feeling a few years before 1983. Looking back, the poem seems almost a premonition.

Abyss
(1980)

To stand on the edge of an awakening
is to tremble blindfolded at the cliff
unable to see what lies the step ahead
but sensing the risk of the abyss.

As fear and promise vie for attention
and the unknown from within

thirsts to join the unknowable without,
the awareness of the Now about to be
is held in hesitation by the Past
pulling like a rope held by Time
riding a horse trotting the other way.

I sense a new vision of reality
and fear the isolation of the knowing
so I remain yet awhile on the edge
knowing I shall never return
knowing I have already leapt.

Chapter 3

THE LIGHT OF BEAUTY

Light invitation
Eternal life
Dissolve to merge
Ecstasy too soon
Return to tell
See Beauty.

The date was January 26, 1983, a Wednesday. I had had a busy day as chemistry administrator at Caltech, followed by teaching a night chemistry class at a city college some distance away. I came home late and very tired—nothing unusual. Nothing, that is, until sometime during the night, when I had a stunning experience. It was wordless, and I was sensing and *knowing* everything in an extraordinary way. My account of it requires I use words, yet to do so instantly shrinks the experience into a description only. I cannot give you the full experience itself. It was all-encompassing, without the edges that words demand.

22

The Light

It seemed I was dreaming, yet I was aware of the position of my body in bed: flat on my back, legs out straight, arms close to my sides. In the distance before me, I saw the silhouette of a mountain. There was a soft white light behind it. On top of the mountain, I saw the side view of a statue of a male angel with wings. He was sitting, facing left to where the mountain began sloping downward. His head, looking down to the ground, was propped with his fist to his forehead and his elbow on his left knee. It reminded me of the position of someone thinking or grieving. Without conscious intent, my awareness instantly zoomed from my body to arrive within a foot of his wings. The image filled my whole visual field. I was amazed at the exquisite detail of the stone. I had never seen anything so clearly as the color and texture of it. Then I suddenly zoomed back to my own body. I was lying in bed, alone as before, with the statue still visible on the distant mountain.

The light behind the mountain began to increase in intensity until nothing but pure white light was present. I was transfixed by the light, awed and motionless. I came later to call it *the light of a thousand suns*. The intensity was beyond all rationality for the human eye to view, yet I could *see* it. It seemed to pulse, and I sensed an invitation to join it.

However, I was hesitant to join, not from fear, but because I felt this might not be a dream. Then a genderless voice spoke as if its source was directly adjacent to, or perhaps inside, my left ear. I had never heard a voice so perfect in tone, quality, and exquisiteness of sound. Without emotion, it said, as if a simple truth, "Eternal life."

23

It seemed to encourage movement toward the light, but I still refrained. It repeated, "Eternal life," and I then began to surrender myself to the light.

From the periphery of my body, semitransparent *bubbles* of my own white light were released. They moved rapidly toward the intense light as they burst open to join it. It was ecstasy! My periphery continued to shrink as it dissolved until the only physical part of me remaining in my awareness was my head and upper torso, centered around my heart. I was about to leave even that behind as I continued to separate from my body. Then thoughts appeared, and I heard myself think with the calm of complete certainty: *This is no dream. This is really happening. I am dying in my sleep. If I continue, I will never return.* The process of mergence paused, with *me* somehow floating between my body and the light. Still in a state of ecstasy, I felt very torn to make a decision. I had an overpowering longing to join with the light; yet my thoughts were, *It is too soon. There is something I must do first.*

So the process gently stopped, and I fully returned to my body as I transitioned back to normal awareness. I was in the same position in the bed as first described. I opened my eyes to see my darkened bedroom. I felt as if the rest of my body was immobilized. There was no fear, only overwhelming serenity within and around me. I very soon fell asleep.

The Red Rose

When I awoke the next morning, I felt changed. I was not the same somehow, but I couldn't understand any of it. Had I been in a mild trance or a hypnagogic state? I didn't know. I only knew I did not want to disconnect from the deep comfort, yet I had to go to work as usual. For several days, everything I sensed seemed different, as if I were in an altered state. Nonetheless, I functioned in my job as usual. I went to bed each night hoping the light would come to visit again. It did not.

In spite of the oddness of the experience, I was not afraid or concerned. I no longer seemed to fear dying. I felt I had been given a gift without knowing what it was or why. And so my inquiry began. It couldn't begin at my workplace at Caltech, where everything was about rationality and logic. What I experienced had neither, and I imagined I would be belittled if I made it known. I simply told my secretary, "I had a strange dream last night, and I'm distracted today."

My real dilemma was that I had had an experience of profound unification that didn't fit at all into my separation scheme!

There was no denying the event had occurred, whatever it was. I must have asked a million questions, even what I had eaten or was doing the day before. It could not have been a drug flashback, as I had never taken any. Nothing made logical sense as a reason. It may have been a dream after all, or an abnormal neurological event within my brain. Maybe I actually would have died. None of that mattered to me. All that was important was the experience of the light. For no specific reason, I never attributed much significance to the angel on the mountaintop. However, the pose of a *thinker* does seem fitting for a scientist!

Within the first few days, I was sitting in my living room when I started looking at a red rose from my yard. I had recently put it in a clear vase across the room. The physical sensations of being so close to merging with the light briefly overcame me. Without doubt, my thoughts were: *The light is still present here, though I am not directly seeing it. It is there, within the beautiful rose. It must be everywhere.* In my mind, I saw that rose as a localized material form that emerged from and was still connected to the all-encompassing light. I felt a realization of the light as the *source* of all beauty, and so I began to call it the *Light of Beauty.* It was a first step toward comprehension of this new reality. Although I had given it the name *Beauty,* I knew the name was inadequate. I capitalized it to identify it as more than the commonplace meaning of the word. I continued to experience unexpected comfort every time I saw anything that was beautiful.

I recorded the event as a poem within a couple days. I consider it consistent in content with my more detailed description above, with the exception that the *fear* was more a low level of *concern.*

The Gift
(1983)

I saw Beauty in the night
as radiance without form
a light of a thousand suns bright.

I was awed, overwhelmed,
as it pulsed its invitation to join
and with absolute clarity
whispered stately in my ear,
"Eternal life, Eternal life."
I thought myself asleep
and safe within a dream

so blissfully surrendered to the union,
and like bubbles of light bursting forth
dissolved from the periphery
and began to merge with the brilliance.

Such ecstasy no words can speak of!

The process almost complete
with little of my self remaining
my mind suddenly grew fearsome
and hesitated.
"This is no dream! This is no dream!
To continue is certain death
and I am not yet ready!"

So with fear I withdrew, as did the light,
and with open eyes and unmovable body
recognized the room
before entering a sleep so deep
for two days I did not fully waken.

And so, on January 26, 1983, at age thirty-nine, the direction of my two paths, science and spirituality, changed from widening separation to the beginning of unification. It started as a subtle shift of direction in response to an intense longing to return to Beauty's presence. I have been travelling for the last thirty-three years with a gift that I am only now ready to share.

Chapter 4

LIVING TWO PATHWAYS: PHASE TWO

1983-2004

Metaphysics tangoes with science
Intimacy of rhythm
Beats the tune
"Divine Living through Chemistry."

New Spiritual Pathways

S hortly after my experience with the Light of Beauty, I searched through books for explanations. It was 1983, and I found little of relevance. What I did find through a friend was a metaphysical spiritual teacher. Even though I didn't know the word *metaphysics,* it didn't take long to discover there were other approaches to interpreting existence than my Catholic upbringing. I was fascinated by the wide range of spiritual systems for finding meaning and comfort in life. I was taught about *energy* centers in the body, meditation, spiritual healing, practices to develop awareness, and other religions besides Christianity. I read and listened, sought the underlying principles, and found my heart often touched. I made no assumptions about absolute Truth, but used my new sense of Beauty as my intuitive guide for value in the lessons.

My metaphysical teacher told me right away not to expect my experience with the Light of Beauty to happen again exactly as before. He said I had to let go of such a desire. Although I was saddened at first to hear this, he was right. The gift was already given, but not so I could inflate myself as *special*; rather, it was to open me to other ways of realizing the Divine through personal spiritual growth.

When my metaphysical teacher moved out of the immediate area, he suggested I pursue my studies with a local group. There was a nearby small spiritual seminary headed by a remarkable woman. The focus was on healing body, mind, and spirit, predominantly by healing touch. I attended lectures and courses with the skepticism of my inner scientist and often cringed intellectually at the absurd lack of logic and rationality. Yet I kept coming back. I often asked myself, *Why am I doing this?* I soon realized it was due in large part to the presence of a group of compassionate people, the majority of whom genuinely wanted to explore spiritually, to deepen their own awareness, and to be of service to others. It was in stark contrast to both the strict, unquestionable beliefs of my childhood Catholicism and the strict, always-questionable facts of my adult science. The group was also composed predominantly of women. Their feminine presence helped balance the isolation I felt working in the male-dominated profession of chemistry.

I continued this involvement until 1989, when I obtained

the degree of Bachelor of Natural Theology in Sacred Healing. I was also ordained a Minister of Healing. I found my heart truly opening as I did the required hours helping strangers who came to the free clinic. I will never forget the man with HIV who had a rash on his right hand that he wanted to heal. It was the mid-1980s, and not much was known yet about the disease. I worked with him, nonetheless, with all the loving-kindness I truly felt. I wasn't at the clinic the following week when he returned. His hand had healed of the rash, and he wanted to have me work with him again. I was unwilling to believe I had actually had anything to do with his hand healing. The healing practice was based on an implicit belief of a connection between compassionate touch and biochemical events. I had no way of knowing if the connection was true and struggled with the concept.

A final paper and public presentation were required for graduation. The theme of mine was based on contrasts between science and spirituality and my search for a middle way. The duality of separation and unification was still operating within me. However, whenever I had a physical sensation of my heart expanding, I knew Beauty was gently present.

As other events in my life took priority, contact with friends made at the healing center gradually slipped away. My spiritual life was still present, but now expanded, freer of imposed rules, and more open-hearted. I continued to reflect, write poems, and occasionally play the piano. Then the time came to rebalance the role of science in my life.

Employment

I was well established in my position as administrator for the chemistry division at Caltech when the experience of the Light of Beauty happened. I was very content in that role as I began my spiritual exploration outside of work. I was able to balance these two aspects of my life and felt my two pathways calmly shifting directions toward each other. All was going well.

I wasn't looking to move from my job. I enjoyed the projects I had, such as converting from manual to computerized systems in the stockroom and secretarial support services. It was a joy and challenge to work with such brilliant people, and I was always treated respectfully. But then in 1986, a headhunter approached me about a job elsewhere, and my life got exceptionally messy. Only in retrospect can I view what happened as a difficult path toward something ultimately wonderful in my life.

In brief, I interviewed for a high-level administrative job at the University of California, Los Angeles (UCLA) for a new institute to be established from ground up. Its goal was to integrate researchers from different disciplines to address broad problems in science—much like a think tank. It all sounded very exciting! After what I thought was a thorough exploration of the details of the position, I accepted the offer.

Within a few months, I fully realized that I had been hoodwinked and that all was not as it seemed. I knew I had to get myself out of that job, but I had to consider my whole situation with regard to finances, housing, and a new job before I could quit. Life was definitely complicated again! I went into survival mode.

31

After a torturous rational consideration of my situation, I finally asked myself the most important question of all: *What do you really want to do in your heart?* I'm not sure I would have even thought to ask that question had it not been for my active association with the healing center. The internal answer was loud and clear: *teach organic chemistry!* At the time, I was in my early forties and hadn't had a full-time teaching job for eight years.

I agonized about all the details. I also realized I had better get busy saving for retirement as a single person. I schemed a risky plan, was scared and insecure, but gave myself two years to try it before reevaluating. I was on a mission to return to teaching. It took all the courage I could find within myself to take each step, and I stumbled many times along the way.

Through a connection made before I quit the UCLA administrative job, I quickly got a teaching position as Visiting Lecturer for one summer course in the UCLA Department of Chemistry and Biochemistry. That opened a significant door. After two years of part-time teaching at UCLA and other schools in the Los Angeles area, I was hired by UCLA in 1989 for a one-year full-time appointment as a Lecturer. I continued with reappointments annually for six years. At that point, due to a union rule, a critical decision had to be made by the department: give me a three-year contract or let me go.

As the department had never had such a three-year position for a Lecturer, they were reluctant to start with me, even though I had already won the departmental teaching award in recognition of my excellent teaching. I put my portfolio together and waited in fear of being denied the position, but finally, I was offered the first three-year contract in the department as a Lecturer of Chemistry. Every three years, I continued until retirement to provide extensive documentation of my teaching activities and waited to see if I still had a job. However, the value of my position to the department became quite clear, and eventually two more Lecturers were hired in similar roles. Along the way, each of us individually won both the departmental teaching award and the esteemed UCLA award of "Distinguished Lecturer." We had a big impact on chemistry education! I like to think I broke new ground in the department when I decided to follow my heart back to teaching.

So if I were to leave out all the distress in the middle of the above history, I could simply say, "I quit my administrative role at Caltech in 1986 and returned to what I loved to do—teaching organic chemistry." I retired as an award-winning Senior Lecturer in 2004 after eighteen years at UCLA. I like to think all the difficult mess in the beginning was just the path to redirect me into teaching again, but specifically at UCLA. I learned eventually why UCLA was so important.

Teaching at UCLA

As with most good jobs, fulfilling primary activities are usually accompanied by often-wearisome chores. Teaching organic chemistry at UCLA required very hard work. I had little time for anything else but work. I was single. My social life was close to non-existent. I couldn't afford to live nearby, so my commute was long and stressful.

Enrollments in my classes were on the order of three hundred students per course, and I usually had two courses per quarter term. I estimated that by the time I retired, my quarterly enrollments totaled over thirty thousand students. Graduate students working toward their advanced degrees were assigned to me as Teaching Assistants (TAs) for each course. They were essential for helping me and the students, and I was very grateful for their contributions.

I taught three different rigorous introductory organic chemistry lecture courses, which changed in content over the years. As organic chemistry is a difficult subject with its own language and symbolism, writing clear lectures was a challenge in scientific communication. I had multiple office hours with groups of students, gave additional reviews before exams, counseled students, managed my teaching assistants, and wrote many letters of recommendation— among other job requirements. It was especially stressful when exams were given. Exams in organic chemistry required drawing chemical structures for many answers. Accurate grading took days of work for the TAs and myself. For a class of three hundred students, final exams could total up to fifteen thousand individual answers to be graded.

It was several years before Excel software was available to record exam scores and calculate course totals for assigning grades. I had no computer or printer in my office for many years. I had to buy my own equipment as well as any specialty software to have at home, and I had to teach myself how to use all of it. There was little or no secretarial help. I felt *outside* the regular department faculty in many ways because I wasn't in a tenure track position. Others in the department decided the course curriculum, but I was free to decide how to present the material.

Enough of difficulties!

Given such conditions, the natural question to ask is: *Why do this job?* The answer for me was clear. I loved organic chemistry, learning about cutting-edge research from the faculty, teaching the large classes—and the students. It was really all about the students! It was a diverse group: different races, religions, countries of origin, educational backgrounds, languages, interests, and more. I was doing what I was meant to do with my talents and reaching a large audience. They, in turn, were teaching me about a cross-section of humanity. For the most part, the department just left me alone to do the work. There were many ways to apply my teaching creativity without interference.

Not long after I started teaching at UCLA, the early Mac computers with their visual-based operating systems became available. Then came software to display organic molecular structures, followed by software to make movies. With these tools, I could envision the direction the future would take for teaching organic chemistry. Both excited and highly motivated, I taught myself what I needed to know in order to make narrated animations of organic structures and reactions to display to the whole class. The large lecture halls were equipped with viewing screens that could project from computer input. Although the work was difficult and time-consuming, the results completely modernized the way I taught organic chemistry. It was thrilling for me to see the students rapt with attention as the language of invisible molecules became visually alive for them during the lecture.

Simultaneously, but separately from UCLA, in 1990 I

started my own business trademarked CHEM TV. I created CDs of my self-narrated animations of organic molecular structural features and reactions. I hired two exceptionally talented programmers, found a publisher to market the CDs to teachers and students elsewhere, and presented the movies at educational conferences. Though they are now outdated due to changes in operating systems, I was proud of those CDs, especially given the technical tools available at the time. It was exhausting and difficult work but exceptionally gratifying.

As a distant aside, during this time, I made a decision to change my last name from my married name. I had thought about it for many years after the divorce but hadn't decided what name I wanted. Then one day, a professor from another university visited me to learn how I was teaching organic chemistry. It turned out he knew my previous husband, and he made a very inappropriate, insulting remark. I decided it was time to get rid of that married name! What I did was make up a new one altogether. After careful reflection, I made a list of seven values I personally hold dear, and made the acronym LUCEIGH. Now, when I write, see, or hear my name, I am reminded of a standard of values for myself. Because I hold it sacred, I have not shared the list with anyone.

Teaching became more difficult physically by my late fifties, and I knew it was time to start planning for retirement. In 1997, I bought seven acres of undeveloped land in the foothills of the Sierra Nevada Mountains in central California. From then forward, I spent the little time I could spare visiting my land and being immersed in its natural expression of Beauty.

Beauty and Chemistry

Being so busy with teaching and my business did not mean I lost all awareness of Beauty and her significance in my life. Rather, she offered deeper expressions.

First of all, over the time I was teaching, computers became powerful *presentation* tools as well as *research* tools. This was especially dramatic to me in the area of biochemical structures— the organic compounds found in living systems. There was not only a seemingly exponential increase in the number of individual structures determined in precise atomic detail, but also an increase in their size and complexity. Visualizing molecular *models* of these real structures became possible through sophisticated interactive computer software. It enabled the viewer to rotate the structure in space, differentiate sub-regions or specific atoms by colors, illustrate the molecular shape in different model formats, and much more. Prior to the availability of such software, hand-held molecular models were the only option.

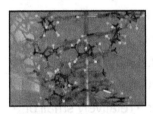

DNA Physical Model, Five Base Pairs

My teaching topics covered biochemical structures, including macromolecular ones, such as proteins and DNA. It was impossible to draw these very complex structures on the board, so I used whatever was accessible to illustrate them. When I first began to teach, I had only a few images available to make into slides. By the time I neared retirement some thirty-five years later, I could bring a computer into the classrooom and select molecular images from thousands available on internet data banks. I could display and manipulate a model on the large lecture room screen for all students to see.

As an analogy, consider maps. Many may still use or remember printed books of maps like the Thomas maps. To find a map, one manually used the index and flipped through pages. The information was limited to what could be printed on the page. Now imagine a modern online Google Maps search: one can select the map of a specific country by typing in the name of the country on the screen, observe the country's overall shape and location on Earth, type in a specific address and zoom into one selected street, and even virtually drive on it. I could do a similar process for molecules. From a molecular data bank, I could choose a biochemical model, whether a relatively small one like the protein myoglobin to an enormous one like DNA. By zooming inside the model of the structure, I could then illustrate specific detailed regional atomic features within the context of the total molecular space. (For a modern link to a databank of biomolecules, search for the "RCSB Protein Data Bank, an Information Portal for over 100,000 Biological Macromolecular Structures." Just browsing will give you a sense of how complex some macromolecules are.)

I felt very fortunate to teach during a time period of extraordinary advances in chemistry. Because of computer-based visualization tools, I could more deeply experience the exquisite Beauty inherent in organic biomolecular structures. Relating the structural features to the molecule's biological function revealed an even deeper connection. The Beauty of exceptionally large molecules was revealed by the unfathomable *complexity* in the details of their atomic connections. Within one whole macromolecule, there can be thousands of atoms uniquely arranged in space due to specific natural bonding forces holding them together.

We may never discover the precise molecular evolution that resulted in the formation of such molecules, nor the process by which some molecules were selected over others to generate living systems. Once life began, however, individual biomolecules had a *function* within a unified, complex system of other molecules. That is, from the totality of its diverse specific atomic connections, each molecule expresses a purpose within a larger system of other molecules. *That community purpose might be described as each molecule's diverse but cooperative participation in the expression and continuation of life.* I find it an astounding realization! (For excellent animations of cellular molecules, visit the site "Harvard Bio Visions.")

My deepening experience of Beauty could be expressed another way. I realized I was looking at models of structures *out there* on a screen that actually existed *in here* in my own living cells! I was using the real molecules within me to look at and understand representations of the same molecules on screen. *I was human life aware of its own molecular parts and their relationships!* I often told my students we were *"using* the molecules we're studying to *study* the molecules we're using."

The level of complexity was so astounding that it left me wordless. It gave me that same feeling as the red rose from long ago. I would think to myself: *These molecules of Life are forms of matter that arose from the all-encompassing Source of Beauty. They took form out of her formless realm in order that Life could express Beauty's essence. Long after the birth of the Universe, atoms were created within stars, then coalesced to create Earth, and ultimately connected to form the Beautiful molecules of Life. Throughout the process, separation moved toward unification at an increasingly complex level.*

I believe knowing the fine atomic details inherent in complex biomolecules was essential to my recognizing Beauty's presence in each molecule as a whole. It also provided a template for imagining the next level of organization. Knowing the details of diversity of individual molecules was essential for my recognizing Beauty's unifying expression in the formation of multi-molecular living systems. To continue this line of thought raises more questions: *If diverse living systems cooperate in a Beautiful expression and continuation of Life, what new life forms might evolve? If diverse cultures cooperate in a Beautiful expression and continuation of Life, what new mega-culture might evolve? If diverse human consciousness cooperates in a Beautiful expression and continuation of Life, what new levels of consciousness might evolve?*

In some odd way, my love of the science of organic chemical structures had come around full circle to touch the heart of my own physical form with its Beauty. *My earlier focused separation moved toward expanded unification.*

Secondly, with regard to Beauty and chemistry, I wanted deeply to share my personal experiences with my students. Yet my job was to teach the science only. That wall of separation learned from my youth was still strongly in place. I truly felt that if I said anything about Beauty or being awed by what we were studying, I would commit a major sin of science and be ostracized to science purgatory!

However, after I had been at UCLA for some time and felt more secure, I could not resist. In the mid-1990s, I ended the last lecture of one term by displaying a few special complex structures and reviewing features of them that the students had learned as preparation for the final exam. Then I dared to speak of how amazing and Beautiful each structure was as a whole. I trembled as I spoke off the script of chemistry, but afterward, my world did *not* crash in!

On the contrary, I got more daring. Given my workload, I had many quarters to have last lectures. Once I read one of my former poems, "The Bird of Morn," as provided at the end of this chapter. I was amazed at the students' response. Perhaps they were surprised by me doing something other than chemistry, namely something *human.* I kept challenging myself to reach for a bigger-picture summarization each term and sometimes included new poems.

During some of those special lectures, I can't really say what my state of awareness was. I loved those students. I wanted them to *know,* in a larger sense of the word, that what they learned had deeper meaning. It was a meaning only available after all the hard work learning the basics. I wanted them to sense the *wholeness* of the subject once they knew the parts. I wanted them to realize that what was true of the *process* of learning organic chemistry was true for other situations in life.

I gained more courage to speak from my heart. There were times when the room was so still, so quiet, everyone so attentive, that I could have heard the proverbial pin drop. I felt like I was talking to Oneness itself and fully connected to them within it. I felt so humbled. I wanted them to experience something beyond our everyday lessons. My longings for them elevated me to a higher state of myself. I often didn't realize the impact until after I finished and saw some students teary-eyed or they came to the front to hug me. I knew I had evoked something beyond carbons and hydrogens within some of them.

In a way, it was as if all my many years of teaching had come to a level of such total integration that it was finally possible to speak in this different way. I never directly shared with them my experience with the Light of Beauty, but I knew Beauty was in the room. I alluded to Beauty whenever I could on those days. I wrote poems to share that included Beauty along with the chemistry. Yet it would not have been possible if I had not already rigorously taught them the foundation upon which to build this awareness. My job at that point was to suggest possibilities of *more,* something that might linger in their imaginations after they completed the course.

Those lectures were not only possible because of preparation through my advanced chemistry education and many years of teaching. They were also possible because of preparation by my metaphysical and healing teachers and years of practicing spiritual awareness. During those lectures, my chemistry and spirituality combined in moments of unity before separating again. I opened to the possibility that unification could happen *within* me if I wanted to transmit it *through* me.

In retrospect, I believe the ultimate lesson of those treasured years was this: *Beauty unites.*

Retirement from Chemistry

I previously hinted that the pathway that led me to teach specifically at UCLA was significant. I think UCLA was special for me for several reasons: allowance for my creative freedom, a large audience to address, a broadening awareness gained from the wide diversity of students, access to leading-edge advancements in chemistry and related technology, and more. UCLA provided a creative atmosphere where I gave my best outwardly and evolved toward greater unification inwardly. Ultimately, UCLA gave me a venue to express and more fully realize Beauty.

Nonetheless, my last few years teaching became increasingly difficult, partly because I was older and it was harder to keep up the physical pace. I also felt I had actualized myself in this arena and knew the time was approaching for a shift. But I know there was more to it than that. I sensed that a new style of student interaction was coming and that I might have a hard time adapting to it.

Technology was not only changing classroom presentations, but also changing students. When students began to use cell phones during a lecture and to use email to ask questions that were unanswerable without a chalkboard to draw on, I felt I could not teach as effectively. Perhaps these indicated a shift in the social dynamic that I highly valued as a major component of successful learning. I began to wonder if I was going to become as outdated as the slide rule I had used at their age!

I had purchased my bare land in 1997. I designed and built a house on it early in 2001. I was happily on vacation working there when the 9/11 attacks happened. As with the Kennedy assassination, every detail of those surreal moments is clear in my memory. I believe the event and our response to it forever changed our country.

When I returned from my vacation and started the new term teaching at UCLA, it was a difficult time for everyone. The following story reflects the emotional state of both me and my students in late September of 2001. The chemistry instructor in the adjacent large lecture hall had planned a demonstration on the first day. I had not been informed of it ahead of time. The demonstration involved a chemical reaction that made an unusually large *boom* noise we could hear in my lecture room. After a collective reflex jerk of bodies, I thought the students were going to rush out of our room, believing it was a bomb. It was my job to calm them, and *me,* after I figured out what had happened. That day was probably one of the most difficult lectures I ever had to give. There was no way to feel normal when the air was thick with the combined grief of students who had lost not only people they knew in the Twin Towers, but also their innocence about our country.

For several years, I frequently visited and worked on my new home until I officially retired from UCLA in 2004 at sixty years old. A spacious haven awaited, a place to explore in the presence of natural Beauty. I still believed I was to teach, but the subject was to change. But to what?

The Bird of Morn
(Written 1980s, shared with chemistry class 1990s)

Asleep in the silent flowered field
Creativity lay dreaming in the dawn,

all calm,
all order undisturbed she quietly lay;
only the first bird of day
moved across the stillness
toward the hill beyond.

She did not know that deep below
Chaos was gathering his forces
so that soon disorder would emerge;
no, unperturbed, she gently turned
upon the first tremble
while the lone bird altered his flight
as if a symbol
of the fright about to be.

Then with a sudden roar
Chaos announced his intent
and his energies more released unbent
shook all forms,
awakening Creativity with a start to see
trees asway,
creatures in panic running away
in frenzied aimless paths, all eyes aghast
at the motion dynamic,
rocks tumbling, water gushing,
fear rushing at the abyss just opened;
the flowered field seemed an ocean
tossing the waves.

Creativity alone stood still and smiled;
she knew
the mass so askew was vulnerable to her vision;
it was her decision to rearrange
what Chaos had unconstrained;
the patterns loosened in his confusion
she remained to form
a new illusion of reasoned order.

Gently she blew the rocks hurling in air
into the abyss, settling there
to accept the water
she raised her hand to show the way to flow
to feed the field awry,
uprooted trees rolling by the hill
she cried to bridge the stream
so creatures might cross
who feared to remain
in the unfamiliar scene.

His energies spent, Chaos retreated,
and Creativity content
gazed at the structure anew in peace
formed from the pieces of his rage;
she was pleased with her partner,
and others were too
for what Creativity
had dared to do.

Calm returned to the air
as did the bird of morn
to drink the water freshly formed into the stream;
he did not ask what did it mean,
nor did Creativity as she ambled away
to find another game to play it seemed
or perhaps again to dream.

Chapter 5

LIVING TWO PATHWAYS: PHASE THREE

2004-2017

Separation
City, home, work
Dispossessed,
Bare land, bare mind
Offer of space
For new connections.

Retirement at Starwater

Separating from my profession, my home, and the Los Angeles area and moving to a small village in the foothills of the Sierra Nevada Mountains made 2004 a year of major changes in my life.

I named my seven-acre property Starwater (StarH$_2$O) for the simple reason that I can look up to see a multitude of stars and look down without interruption to see the water of the river far below. I have a logo to represent this—a large one in metal at my front door.

Starwater Logo

As previously mentioned, once I had bought my bare land in 1997, I came to visit it as often as possible. Frequently, I would just walk around or sit on a rock and enjoy being simply present among the natural scenery. I know those visits influenced my insights and openness in writing meaningful closing lectures for my organic chemistry students. Here is one of the first poems I wrote while being at Starwater before the house was built and before I retired and moved there permanently.

A Piece of Land
(1998)

It's only a piece of land,
one dot on the planet,
one parcel,
seven acres,
thousands of square feet,
millions of square inches.

Only a piece of land.

The dirt disturbed by insect, deer, or rain
waits to become a foundation,
trees with long-dead limbs
wait to be styled or yearn to be awakened by water;
and rocks hold their steady vigilance
eager for the change of scene.

Only a piece of land.

What has drawn me here is already its own story,
what will keep me here has yet to be written,
but what will be discovered and cherished
is already shouting joyfully of its opening.

Homeless too long in houses alone,
the need overtakes me
to join the only love that will not leave until I do,
Earth beneath.
Unheld too long, it holds me,
untouched too long, it gives itself into my hands,
unseen within, it lets me see without,
gives me views beyond my limitations,
gives me space sought, so long sought,
to merge once again with the Light.

But is it selfish to want so much for my own soul?
A place of Beauty
in a world splattered with the grotesque,
a place of calm
among the agonized cries of the suffering?
Who am I to wish this abundance for myself?

Yet some part within seems to know
a clear certitude of a purpose to fulfill,
of so much more I have to give,
of my best waiting for release,
of an explosion of the deepest and most essential,
that cannot occur without self-destruction
unless I am part of

only a piece of land.

I map my changes over my first twelve years of retirement
as a sequence of steps: change location → change context

→ change influences → change choices → change thoughts, emotions, behaviors → change consciousness.

Adaptation was required for all of these changes. Challenges have been ongoing, as has been the relentless aging of my body! My pathway of change has been daily impacted by several basic influences: living in the country in a small village, making social connections, and developing intellectually and spiritually.

Country Living

The Los Angeles area population is on the order of four million people. My last eighteen years there, I lived in a suburb in a small house with barely any land around it. I was close enough to my neighbors to hear them talking inside their house. I had a long commute to UCLA. Most of my normal views were of other small houses, stores, and freeways. Occasionally, I could see a star or, if lucky, a glimpse of the moon. I heard city noises everywhere.

I now live in a village of about twenty-six hundred people. Most of the properties are multiple acres, along with some smaller neighborhoods and very large ranches. Several rivers run through the widespread community, and there are mountains and foothills to be viewed everywhere. Through the village runs a two-lane, six-mile stretch of our main highway without any stop signs or lights. We have at least one of any store or service that might normally be needed. Otherwise, the nearest medium-size city is about thirty miles away.

Black Bear by Road

Western Owl in Oak Tree

My nearest neighbors are wild creatures: snakes, spiders, deer, raccoons, bobcats, foxes, bears, and all manner of birds. For me, the seasons are marked by whether it's too cold or too hot for the rattlesnakes! It's a thrill, as well as a potential danger, to drive around a curve and have a deer or bear meandering on the road, or to find a mother bear and her cub clinging to a tree near my deck! My nearest human neighbors are acres away, but some houses are visible through the oak trees and on the mountain slopes across the river.

Located up a hillside, I have an uninterrupted panoramic view of more than a hundred and eighty degrees.

View from Top of Starwater, River Below

At night, I see the Milky Way and literally billions of stars. I watch the moon and sun rise from behind the mountain across the valley. I see breathtaking sunrises and sunsets on clouds in the sky. I hear the variety of sounds from the long stretch of river as the water level rises or falls. I feel the wind blow up-valley and down-valley almost every day. My house has a continuum of large picture windows to make me feel I'm always outside and a deck so I can literally be there. All of this provides something very important to have around me: a *natural, spacious environment.*

My only incoming physical services are a phone landline and electricity. I have a well for water, a village cell tower for computer and cell phone connections, and a tank of propane for heat. I gave up TV satellite transmission willingly five years ago but have satellite radio. I have learned to do many of the simpler house repairs on my own. I have a utility vehicle to get around the property to do tasks. I hire helpers as needed. All of this has taken years to set up and figure out.

I assume it is obvious that my country life is very different from my former city life. The natural setting, with its diversity of visual offerings and interactions with wildlife, has had a profound impact on me.

Country Pets and People

There is a rich variety of domesticated animals in this village: horses, cows, goats, llamas, and many dogs and cats. It's a joy to drive along and see large animals grazing in pastures. It's not such a joy when cows get loose and block the road.

Ribo Puppy

I rescued a dog one year after I retired. His name is Ribo, as in riboflavin or ribonucleotide—hey, I'm still a chemist! He is the love of my life, a mix including greyhound, very sweet-natured, with a natural smile.

Ribo and Luceigh in Wildflowers
Photo by Alaura Shouse

When he looks straight into my eyes and holds his gaze, it's like he sees my very soul, though often he probably simply sees a way to get a treat. We take care of each other in our different ways. Ribo uses his keen canine senses to alert me to anything coming onto the property, day or night. He is my protector and huggable companion. He listens to me talk and sometimes does his funny best to talk back. I love to watch him as he runs freely around the property during the day—no cages or fences. I value his freedom of movement as if it were my own. It's great to be able to take Ribo with me into some of the local stores and the post office. Even the bank has dog treats to offer when he comes in.

Getting to know people was a bit more complicated, of course. It helped, during the time I was visiting my property and building my house, to get acquainted with a few local residents and workers. Once I moved here, people were generous about introducing me to other people, who then introduced me to others. It also helped that many were retired and wanted social contact as well. It is really wonderful to go to the market or post office, bump into someone you know, and have a short chat to stay in touch. I finally learned that it's okay to say, "Hi, what's new with you?" Over time, I have come to feel part of a community, a feeling I never really had living over twenty-five years among four million people in Los Angeles.

Participating in community activities has been an important way to sustain social connections. Here are a few examples: I was an electric keyboard player in a small band for several years; I've shared events with other authors, such as book signings and readings; I've taken Pilates and drawing classes; I've presented performance poems at our local "Concert on the Grass." A couple in the village started the Performing Arts Institute that has brought exceptionally talented musicians and performers to our small village. There are many other options always available within the village community. One can also choose to do none of them. One personal project, especially meaningful to me, was going through my collection of poems written since my teenage years. I selected a representative group and published a book in 2011, *Posit Poems: A 50-Year Collection from an Inquisitive Heart.*

Spiritual and Intellectual Growth

There are two group activities that have been of special significance to me for many years now.

One, surprisingly, is due to a connection from my days at the healing center in the 1980s. After more than twenty years, it was remarkable to me to find people who had studied with the same healing teacher. A woman about my age in a small town not far from where I live has an informal group that meets monthly for meditation, spiritual discussion, and shared learning. I am deeply grateful to participate in a group of people who explore and share spiritual awareness and growth. I have known them now for over ten years and value their friendships and the deepening of my spiritual life their interactions have supported.

The other important activity is one I started in 2010 called the Brain Group. We are six to eight women in our mature years with a common goal to keep our brains active and healthy through learning. We use recorded lecture courses and other online resources. After watching presentations, we have lively discussions on the subject. We have studied such courses as neuroscience of the brain, cosmology, history of life on Earth, philosophy, developmental psychology, memory, music and the brain, the aging brain, and many more! This group not only is about the stimulation of our intellects by learning new topics but also has a highly valued social component as we age.

I find it remarkable that I have both a significant spiritual group and a significant intellectual group to enrich my life in retirement. I never dreamed when I first bought my land twenty years ago that I would participate in these two groups, each focusing on an aspect of my own *separation*. I have learned deepening lessons of unification from each of them.

Personal Integration

Over my retirement years, I have expanded my spiritual awareness beyond healing and broadened my overall science knowledge well beyond chemistry. I have had the opportunity to integrate these two paths of knowledge in my life without any reason to keep one secret from the other. It has influenced my writing, my interactions with people, and my experience of being human. I don't know that these two paths can ever become one, for they are based on different fundamental premises and methods. Their differences are their strengths and, when recognized as two contributions to a single path of human longing, serve us better by not being pitted against each other or misused by one in a misunderstood effort to prove the other. I need *both* my reasoning mind and my spiritual heart.

The separation-unification theme has followed me into my retirement years. Am I any closer to releasing separation in favor of unification? Where is Beauty in my life now?

One place is in the early morning clouds.

Sunrise at Starwater

* * *

Poems of Nature

Spring Blooms

Spring
(2011)

snowmelt flows
onto green earth-skin
tattooed with fiddlenecks
and lupine
playing with hummingbirds
as the rising sunlight
sits on the wet wooden bench
empty in its waiting
for this first day of spring

Come Closer
(1999)

Atop a barren hill I stood, before the gentle wind,
when first I heard the murmur riding on its wings.
I felt the tender sounds touch upon my skin
to lift question marks embedded in my being.
"Come closer, come closer," it said

as if an invitation to be embraced by its serenity.
Yet no source could I see for my steps to begin
so I silently remained in the breeze.

"Come closer, come closer to understanding," it said.
"Step out from the whirlwind of your confusions."
The chaos of my mind surrounded me poised
to tilt the balance of my trembling illusions.

"Search for structure in disorder presumed.
Make connections one to the other.
What seems misplaced to you now
are but the corners of patterns to discover."

The breeze slowly changed directions
then engulfed me once again,
and I wondered what lesson was I to learn
from this pleading of the wind.

For a long moment I stood in these reflections
when "Come closer, come closer," it said once more.
"Step forward in your quest for freedom
for you have yet to choose your core."

"To unchain the Beauty of the thousand suns
discard all that distorts your view,
for what you select in the clarity of its light
will abundantly appear in you."
I had not sensed till those words
the passing cloud that blurred my visions
and I wondered if the outcome of understanding
was the freedom of conscious decisions.

The breeze quickly became a southern wind
blowing its warmth against my breast.
It was then I became aware of a chill within
and the longing for the voice of this guest.

"Come closer, come closer to true compassion.
Blind judgments have frozen your heart.
For the goal of understanding and freedom
is to unravel complexity apart."

I was overwhelmed by now with the need to move
and lifted one foot from the ground
but I held it there as I sought to know
what was the direction of the sound?

The breeze had stopped; I heard no more
of understanding, of freedom, of compassion.
No more did sounds arrive with the wind
while I waited in my hesitation.

My first step came down before I realized
the murmurs were teachings for my soul.
I knew then the source of the voice was within
saying, "Come closer, come closer to home."

"Every step toward understanding,
every step that is truly free,
every step that moves with compassion
is a step closer to who you will be."

"Come closer, come closer, come closer ..."

A Wolf-Cub-Born-Blind
(c. 1995)

Once a wolf-cub-born-blind
was taught by his kind
the chase of the pack.
All assumed he could see as they
as clumsily he strove to catch the prey

61

not knowing even himself inside
what was absent through his eyes.

The leader lamented his lack of kill
and angrily howled at him until
the valley filled with the young cub's tears,
not understanding what had brought such sneers.

Then one night the wolf-cub-born-blind
heard a lion approaching behind,
steps far distant as the others slept.
He quickly dried the tears he'd wept
and howled a warning to wake the pack.
He saved them all
by what they lacked.

Sun-Dog Focus
(2005)

The sun, about to appear over the mountain peaks,
mirrors its pastel reflections on the clouds.
I am uplifted by their transcendent beauty.
Uplifted, that is, until my dog's whine
shatters my skyward focus.
I turn my stare from the edge of the sun's brilliance
to meet his dark, brown eyes
begging for my assistance.
He wants a chewy. I go get it.

Believing I can then return
to the glorious breaking forth of the morning's light,
I sit quietly again by the window.
My eyes observe that pastels
have now turned to white,
while my ears observe
the gnawing of my dog's teeth

on the grey hoof of a pig.

I may yearn to be transported by the sunrise
to my Higher Self,
but my happy friend is content
in the now of his canine instincts.
Relentless, I focus again on the sunlight
passing through my window,
only to discover its beams ultimately shine
not on me, but on paws of spotted beige.

I wonder if I misunderstand the nature of focus.
I always associate it with restricting concentration,
eliminating distraction, defining boundaries.
But as I watch both sunrise and dog,
I see each intently expressing its essence
as co-participators in the flow of morn.
The sun does not stop for the chewing,
nor the dog stop for the rising.

Perhaps this is my misconception:
to believe I am limited
to view only sunrise or only dog in any moment
rather than expand my vision to embrace them both,
dog as part of sunrise, sunrise as part of dog,
a unified sun-dog focus.

Suddenly the dawning
is no longer about the light of the sun,
but about the enlightenment of my soul.
For perhaps, after all, it is just this:
the ultimate focus
is the vision of nothing separated.

Chapter 6

BEAUTY NOW

A thirty-three- year mystery
Forgetting not an option
The question appears
To an answer given
Unrevealed.

It has been thirty-three years since my experience of
the Light of Beauty. I continue to feel a long thread of
deep connection to her. The sense of her presence at
times seems almost gone, at other times very near. I have
given attention over these years to themes of mergence,
integration, wholeness, and unification. I have longed so
deeply to experience her with the same intensity again,
but she has visited in more subtle ways. Beauty remains
a mystery to be explored.

So much has happened in my life since 1983. I have
used the time to uncover past traumas, handle my innate
anxiety levels, and heal psychological wounds. I have
thought more about what science really can and can't offer
to our knowledge of existence. My spiritual awareness has
grown, waned, grown broader, waned, grown deeper. I

feel now as if all these changes needed to happen before I could more fully experience what is called by different names: Absolute Reality, Truth, Oneness, or, for me, Beauty.

Beauty has been my cherished guide, my touchstone of faith, and my teacher of the ultimate connection to the All-That-Is.

Since my retirement, the revelations of Beauty have accelerated. Living in the natural environment of the country provides a constant reminder of the presence of Beauty through natural forms: sunrises and sunsets, rainbows, snow-capped mountains, expansive clouds. I am reminded frequently of my Oneness with all of it. Through my spiritual group, I have been exposed to new ways of approaching consciousness of the *Whole*, have had opportunities to exchange evolving spiritual teachings, and have been challenged to what might inhibit my fuller awakening. Through my Brain Group, I have broadened my base of knowledge of the universe, the earth, living forms, the brain, the arts, and more. What all of these have in common is making *connections.* I have left the narrow confines of a *Texan/Oklahoman-American-Catholic* little girl and joined the complexity of a global humanity with all its diversity of forms and commonalities of universal longings.

I was unable to interpret what happened in 1983 at that time. In my pursuit of understanding since then, the explanations have been changing as I have matured. It has been an evolutionary process, so at any one time I can only express what I understand in that moment. I have tried to capture ideas and feelings through writing poetry and essays. They help me see where I've been and provide clues for where I am going.

I came to some realizations about my search for a *true* self when I wrote the following poem.

Treasure Found
(2006)

If one moment from now I were to find
the treasure that is my True Self,
what then?
I already know how to search for it,
seek out books and wise ones.
I know how to probe and gather
and connect and theorize.
I am well practiced in the Art of Questing,
know all the moves of the seeker,
but when have I ever rehearsed being still
in the presence of any Gift?

When I find my treasure
will I know how to replace movement forward
with no movement at all?
Will I have my senses tuned to experience it?
Will I know how to be with it in moments of Now,
gently, reverently, completely?
Will I know how to participate in life with the Gift found
and no Great Search remaining to attend to?

If I were to pretend
I already hold the Gift of my True Self,
what insights would be revealed?
Would longing be replaced with acceptance?
Would the answer no longer require the question?
Would I close my books and shred my theories?

Perhaps, after all, it would be just this:
if I were to pretend my True Self is ever present,
I would then realize the actual pretend
had been that it wasn't.

When I wrote and created a YouTube movie titled *Toward WE* (2014), I let something deep within me simply flow without evaluating the meaning as it did. I wrote ideas that I did not understand until afterward, if then. I came up against deep, hidden fears and had to stop the writing until I could identify the problem. I have opened a new door to my inner life, have grown in courage, and have every intention of entering the room waiting for me. I believe this is why I am writing this work now.

Sometime around 2014, I had several brief experiences that I interpreted as Beauty revealing in my mind's eye a sliver of her Light in order to encourage me toward something still unidentified. More recently, during meditations, I have felt Beauty participating within the imagery of the meditation.

It occurred to me that perhaps Beauty had taught me long, long ago what I needed to know. For example, in 1983, I began to dissolve as bursting bubbles of light merging with Beauty. That experience now seems a lesson or practice to let go of myself (i.e., my *small* self) and send the essence of my intentions to merge with a greater reality. I still ask myself if my imagination has made all of this up and created these scenes that are unreal. Yet I do feel there can be unconscious truths that seek ways into our images and words so that we can grasp their reality in our human way. I can't see that it really matters what I feel if they offer me a meaningful course of action in my life: one that is expanding, embracing, connecting ... and Beautiful.

Throughout the last thirty-three years, perhaps my longing for Beauty was the motivation to discover answers to questions like, *Who am I? Who observes me observing the world? Is there anything that exists that I am not connected to in some way? Why is there something rather than nothing?*

Or perhaps, it was *not* that I have been trying to discover the answers to these questions. Perhaps, instead, Beauty had already given me the answers, and I have been trying to discover the questions that need to be asked to reveal them.

The most important question in this moment of my life sounds so simple on the surface, but it has become the most meaningful question of all:

"Is it Beautiful?"

* * *

When Did My *self* Leave?
(2016)

When did my self leave?
Was I asleep somewhere as it happened?
When did my hands reach
to give a caress,
not take a receipt,
my arms open in joyful welcome,
not cross before my chest?

When did I start to cry
at the news of starved refugees
as if they were all at my front door,
feel compassion even for the terrorists
as if their blindness opened my eyes?

Where has my resentment gone?
Has it joined blame, pride, lust, and anger
in an quiet mass extinction of resistance?

To whom did I surrender
the concept of my separated form
as awareness arose within me
of Universal Connectedness?

There was no public decree for my self to leave,
no drama enacted to be witnessed.
I must have been asleep with life's memories
before awakening without their requirement.

My feet walk differently now,
my soles always touching Kindness,
all surface below them the Ground of Being
every path traveled lighted by Beauty,
always at Home already present.

Whether my small self will return for visits,
I cannot say nor am I concerned.
For I still *AM,* my true Self becoming exposed,
realizing what left was only a mistaken identity.

PART II

POEMS AND REFLECTIONS

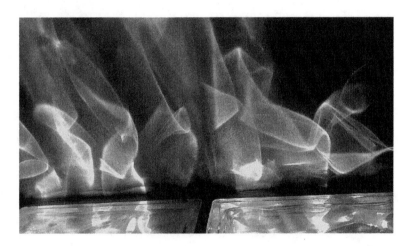

Light through Glass

Remember we differ,
you and me,
simply by what
we choose to see.

Chapter 7

FIVE POEMS

Introduction to "The Longing"

As I adapted to my new life in retirement, I spent many early mornings and late evenings sitting on my deck with my dog Ribo, enjoying the Beauty of my natural surroundings. Especially during those times, I often had such an inexplicable longing arise. I decided one day to write down what was stirring within me. This is what was.

The Longing
(2006)

In the beginning,
did the Universe so long to expand
that it could not refrain from bursting forth,
exuding its contents into the emptiness of potential,
allowing energy to shape-shift into matter,
birthing laws as it birthed forms,
permitting energy to establish
the cosmic rules of order
to balance the drive to disorder,
all the while exhaling the great Question

relentlessly surging ahead of its Answer.

Did freedom only become aware of itself
as it selected out of the swirling choices,
to create a galaxy or something other,
a star or something other,
a planet or something other,
until flecks of matter were condensed
into this Earth-sphere among spheres
so the story might continue to unfold the longing,
still unscathed through all mutations of violence.

Did our humanity evolve
in response to this longing,
so it could be reached for with our arms,
followed with our steps,
reflected upon, written about,
argued over with our words.
Did this longing organize our DNA to yearn for it,
or reserve a secret cell within our hearts
to receive its signal,
so we might all one day recognize
its universal intimacy.

We dreamed up our myths
to acknowledge
this longing that never ceases,
so we might be sustained
by the whys of imagination
until science could measure and explain
the what and how and when and where.

Yet knowledge of facts and theories expands so fast
we are bereft of the simplicity
of our humanity's childhood
and strive to translate our magic beliefs
into even more contorted shapes,

rather than risk
merging ourselves with the longing
or transforming ourselves
into something more profound.

What a force this longing is
to never tire of its Question.
How patient this longing is to wait for us
as we evolve through our ignorance
and misguided substitutes for truth,
as if the longing already realizes
our enlightened freedom will emerge one day
and self-lead our consciousness
into its next expansion,
as if the longing realizes
its birthing continues through us
and we have been participating
since the beginning
in the creative unfolding
of the eternal Answer.

What could we become that has never yet been,
if we would only integrate
what knowledge provides
and spirit guides.
What could we become,
if we would gently accept
all we have passed through
rather than cling in fear
to our most current manifestation.
What could we become,
if we would transmute
beyond our self-imposed restrictions,
and make a leap in conscious development
of such magnitude
that it surpasses
the day the first light shone out of the darkness,

the day the first star was born,
the day the first cell came to life.

Perhaps, just perhaps, that day
we will realize that we, too,
are part of the unfolding Answer
to the Longing's first bursting forth.

* * *

Introduction to "My Vision of Beauty"

Not long after I retired, I knew I wanted to start writing. For several years (2006-2010), I attended an annual "write retreat" of Stanford alumni held at Lake Tahoe, California. One year, I was restless during the night, couldn't sleep, didn't really know why I had come in the first place, and so, about three a.m., I decided to just get up and write something, anything! I sat in the dark silence with only the light of my computer screen and wrote this poem about Beauty. I did not question the words as they came and did very little editing lest I lose the message it held for me. I was longing so deeply to experience Beauty's presence again after more than twenty years.

My Vision of Beauty
(2009)

I saw Beauty in the night
as radiance without form,
the light of a thousand suns bright.
She offered her vision to my unprepared mind,
on its own too small to contain her brilliance.

As she pulsed her invitation to surrender,
I accepted her wordless mergence so complete
there could be no ecstasy greater to surpass the gift
of being nothing into nothing, all into all,
self into the Source of Self.

Even so, as my structure dissolved
to enter Beauty's realm,
I knew somehow it was not yet the time
to stay forever disembodied
or erratically spark my temporal lobe,
but rather to return to the constraints of my form,
return behind the veil of material forces
that must shade Beauty's radiance
lest her intensity evermore disable
my earthly comprehension.

Why, Beauty, why
why touch me so, only to leave me untouchable,
why reveal yourself so,
only to leave me a greater mystery.
Where are you now, radiance of Beauty,
that I cannot reach into the bliss of your fullness,
only seek fragments
through your reflections everywhere:
flower and stream and child,
simplicity and innocence and compassion,
knowledge and understanding and acceptance.

How can I live, Beauty, so filled with your offering
and not pass on the overabundance of it,
tender assurances to other hearts
lest they despair in their illusions
of your absence or temporariness in their lives.
How do I explain what defies the limitation of language
as I learn to transcend the limitations
of my own resistance to serve you.

How do I explain that you imbue forms
to lure us beyond our human weakness,
draw us away from violence and fear,
that all may one day be embraced
in the shared wellspring of your glow.

I have learned to return to you, Beauty,
when I choose to behave Beautifully,
when I choose to see the Beautiful
in living and nonliving,
when I choose to allow the Beautiful
to flow through me,
as when I strive to create an expression
of your reality
and release it freely for all of us,
not as my own but from you,
in hope others will be likewise transformed
as together we evolve
into ultimate reunion with you.

* * *

Three Poems Observing Nature

Immobility
(2014)

The oak tree stands
where a woodpecker dropped an acorn in transport
a random site
dirt and moisture for a womb
under the sun's light.
Its roots record the oak's birthplace
and bestow trunk immobility for a lifetime
a small piece of earth having its hold.

The oak tree before me now,
tall and wide and dense
displays its history in patterns of branches
memories of past joys and heartaches
a record of storms and droughts and nesting birds
now offering shade for my protection.

The tree I call mine has known little violence
perhaps a branch broken by an overweight raccoon
the surgical cut of a limb endangering my roof.
But what of other trees I saw in the news this morning?

The one uprooted to pave a parking lot?
The one blown to sawdust by a war's bomb?
The one with a raped young woman hung on it?
The one standing lifeless above an outdoor school
of young children being taught how to kill?

My tree witnesses my human appreciation,
others are immobile to run from humanity's brutality.
What stories do they report by their bends and breaks?
Did they exude tears from their bark
or scream to shake a branch onto an assassin's head?

Are trees one measure of humanity's
impact on all of life?
Can we simply look at the trees, the immobile trees,
to learn from them what they have experienced us do?
Have we encouraged their lives
nurtured their inherent beauty
or slapped them relentlessly
to affirm our power over them?

My tree before me now
tells me in some strange way
of its relatives across the earth
tells me of their messages sent by the wind.

My tree reminds me
we are both part of a larger living family
in a world in danger of imbalance to an extreme.
It reminds me in our peaceful moment together
that many others are not so.

I am grateful that the acorn dropped here
at the birthplace of the tree I call mine
the tree whose immobility within soil
has so deeply moved within my heart.

* * *

The Tree and I
(2016)

When I am gone from Earth,
ashes spread,
and others sit as I now do,
on the deck of my country home,
will the same oak trees, sensing them, remember me,
remember how I trimmed their dead branches,
enjoyed their shade,
watched the woodpeckers steal their acorns,
exchanged stares with a camouflaged owl?

After I am gone from Earth,
will these trees hold memories of me
locked in their trunks?
Are they recording me in cellulose
as we share today's sunrise?
Someday when I am long forgotten by humans
and a tree near this deck ages and dies,
maybe someone sitting where I now sit will cut the wood

and find inner rings of memories labeled
"Betty lived here."

After the wood is finally burned,
ashes spread,
then no one will ever know
that in this present time by then long past,
the tree and I coexisted
and cherished our precious living moments
together.

* * *

Coexistence
(2014)

A gentle country morning
I sit upon my deck
among motionless leaves,
my dog lies in wait
of a fox or deer to chase,
a woodpecker squawks obscenities
to a finch on his branch,
the thirsty river below
hums a shallow tune,
and the sun's first rays of morn
peek over the mountaintop beyond
and cast stories in its shadows
upon surfaces nearby.

A gentle country morning
I am peaceful, calm,
till a bee seeks entry in my coffee,
my mug, however, covered,
spurred by scary stories

of those who drank before they looked
but the bee flies elsewhere
my fear on its back.

My eyes move downward
to a shadow near my foot
a colorless hummingbird in profile
cautiously approaches
my dog's water bowl
he shares generously.

I sit in wonder
at this great mystery
of coexistence:
dog and bee
sun and shadows
squawks and hums
… and me.
I read the signals
through my senses
remembering our interdependence.
For there would be no experience
of my own existence
if nothing else were there
on this gentle country morning.

Chapter 8

REFLECTION 1:
THE ANSWER BEFORE THE QUESTION

The Birthmark
(1977)

*Our common birthmark as humans
is the question mark
of what it means "to be."*

I n the month before I wrote the first word of this book, I
had an unusual feeling tickling my brain. I sensed I had
an answer within me, unconsciously, without images or
words. An answer, but no question! How puzzling! It was
counterintuitive to feel that an unidentified answer within me
was possible before I even asked the question. It seemed
in this case the question was necessary to draw something
forth from a mix of hidden components in my brain. I felt
certain that if I asked the right question, *something* would
come together naturally into my consciousness.

So I asked myself, "How do I discover the question to
ask?" It seemed I had to ask what question to ask! I could
see the possibility of this quest of questions spiraling into

complete ambiguity if it expanded into too many questions. On the other hand, I might also spiral into one specific question if I narrowed each one along the way. This made me wonder if my mind just wanted to lure me into paradox games!

I decided to take a different approach from mind logic and explore from my heart instead. I did this by meditating with the intention to be open to whatever question might present itself. I didn't find it easy to detach from the mind-chatter. My mind was a huge hip-hop jam session of words and images. I was about to end the meditation out of growing frustration when a banner floated across my inner mind's eye. It was in front of all the blurred confusion. The banner clearly strung the words, "Is it Beautiful?" Immediately I thought, "That's it! That's the question!" It was such a simple, direct question. My heart just knew somehow that this was the one to draw forth the answer I already knew but had not yet expressed. I suspected the question was in my heart in the first place, and maybe it was my heart that was tickling my mind to pay attention.

More questions have presented themselves since then, but they seem to flow on a pathway strewn with answers that invite me to unify them, like flowers to gather into one bouquet. I believe it is my pathway of Beauty leading to unification.

I began to wonder if my experience of the Light of Beauty had actually rewired my brain, creating dormant answers of existence for me to discover as I moved forward with my life from that point. Certainly, there have been multiple small awakenings along the way to the present moment, more frequent in recent years.

Since retirement, I have pursued a strong interest in brain neuroscience. Part of my pursuit of internal unification embraces what is being learned about brain structure and function. My enjoyment of science has not waned as I have explored the mysteries of being a spiritual human. In fact, the combination has given birth to a new understanding of what it means to *be*. I do not have one all-inclusive answer to offer at this moment and doubt that's the point. I have been doing a kind of spiritual research by simply being in a situation and asking myself in that moment, "Is it Beautiful?" The *it* varies. The question encourages me to become aware of a variety of expressions of Beauty arising from the one Source of all Beauty.

In one group meditation around this time, our intention was to connect to, or pray for, those who are suffering around the world. As soon as we started the silent meditation, I was taken aback at how fast my awareness dropped from my mind into my heart. It was as if I were watching a dream movie. I *traveled,* so to speak, by zooming across the planet to the Middle East, where I encountered a woman holding a small child. Both were hungry and afraid. We looked into each other's eyes, and I said to her, "May you find amidst all your sorrows one vision of Beauty each day. May it remind you that you are not alone and give you courage and comfort." I zoomed immediately back to my real body, which was nearly sobbing by then. I did what I needed to get grounded—I breathed.

However, I was still in a meditative state, and I didn't stay long before I zoomed again to some distant part of the planet to find a terrorist about to rape a woman. I came up to him from behind, and he turned his head and looked at me in surprise. I could see the terror in the woman under him, and I could see his anguish as well. He hesitated to continue his action. I said to him, "Look into that woman's eyes and see her fear. You are the cause of her fear. You know your own deepest fear and how that feels. Why would you do that to her? The next time you want to rape a woman, look directly into her eyes and remember *her* fear is yours." I then zoomed back to my own body. I was very surprised to find myself tearful with compassion for that rapist who did not comprehend the horror of his own actions.

I realized that the odd *travel-by-zooming* was similar to when parts of my body were dissolving as bubbles to merge with the Light of Beauty. I could not help but wonder if Beauty had taught me then how to connect to other people in this way and still return to my own self. It all felt so mysterious, yet familiar. I knew I was in an altered, meditative state, but what unfolded was an expansive opening of my heart. It was emotionally similar to my surrendering to the Light of Beauty.

The meditation was beautiful. It left me realizing I can open my spiritual heart and still embrace my intellectual mind. Both are aspects of my beingness. Both can cooperate or can function independently as appropriate to situations.

But mind and heart are not the whole of me. There is something far wider and deeper that both embraces them and is itself embraced by so much more.

Is it, this something else, also Beautiful?

Perhaps I already have the answer.

Chapter 9

REFLECTION 2:
ANSWERING "IS IT BEAUTIFUL?"
AT THE SEASHORE

The Beauty that invited my mergence into her Oneness may not be as clear to recognize as the common meaning of the word *beauty.* Some aspects of the Light of Beauty might include words or phrases that seem to defy any simple explanation: the formless Source of form, the still Source of processes, Infinite Presence, Pure Existence, the Interconnectedness of All-That-Is, or the Boundless.

Without having an actual experience described by such terms, it may seem impossible to answer the question "Is it Beautiful?" in the sense of "Is it full of the Light of Beauty?" Even though we may have an unidentified *felt-sense* that stirs our aesthetic response to what seems beautiful, bringing it into more direct awareness deepens its meaningfulness.

In the summer of 2016, I had an opportunity to spend a week at a house on a pristine stretch of ocean beach along the coast of northern California. As I walked along the beach, I reflected on what it means to answer the question "Is it Beautiful?" when posed in that setting. I invite you to walk with me as you read.

Beauty on the Beach

Northern California Coast, 2016

I walk alone along a limited-access stretch of beach. It is a cool, early morning, and a foggy mist embraces everything. There are precipitous cliffs to my right, outcroppings of rock formations in the waters to my left. The Pacific Ocean stretches away from me as if infinity is just beyond the hidden horizon. Some of the ocean waves hit the rocks and splash random white patterns high in the air as if waving *good morning* to the sky; others make their way gently to the damp shore, inviting the sandpipers to breakfast. I hear the waters' unpredictable patterns of sounds; roars, whishes, and booms create a melody played parallel to my path. Seagulls contribute their cries to the music as they fly just above the water. I see a seal swimming not far offshore, its head turned steadily toward me as if I am the curiosity here. I feel soft moisture whispering on my face, feel the shifting of sand under my shoes. With its variety of forms and processes, the whole experience involves my senses and brings me calming pleasure. I am aware I am having an experience of the present moment. I simply *know* it is Beautiful.

As I reflect more deeply, I begin to notice connections. At first, they are simple: the seal connected to the water, the rocks to the sound of splashes, the sand to the earth, the mist to my face, and my shoes to the shore.

I then observe the connections become broader: the wave over the rocks stirs sand and creatures in the ocean, the seal's head moves up and down with the passing wave front as it observes me observing it, the mist from the ocean travels in the gentle breeze to mix with my breath and enter my body, and I exhale to all before me.

My awareness begins to broaden even further into a vast, inclusive connectedness. I am the observer of all these objects, their forms and motions and contacts and interplays. The information is coming as packets into my senses, but it is more than the sight of water, more than the sound of waves, more than the touch of wind on my skin or the smell of decaying kelp. It is all of them in this moment, all connected with me, all of us in the Now. Even beyond that awareness, there is yet more, for it is not merely the awareness of a set of organized, identifiable objects. There is a feeling, a very deep feeling without words, a feeling that holds everything before me together as one experience—ocean, rocks, sand, seagulls, mist, wind, and one human being. I am not a separate entity, but part of the whole. Within this experience, we are all merged, all experiencing a single event embracing us. We are all harmoniously free, sharing a moment of unification.

This is an experience of Beauty. This is to look through a door ajar to glimpse at the Infinite Presence. My answer to the question in this walk along the beach is, *Yes, this is Beautiful!*

Yet these are my words, only words. The reader can have an experience of my words, but not of the ocean scene itself without personally being there. How I long for every human to have such an experience with Nature somewhere, sometime! I sense somehow that if we truly could share the Light of Beauty within such experiences, we would be better able to participate in creating a more Beautiful humanity. As I have noticed before, *Beauty unites.*

The Cage on the Ocean Beach

I walk on the same stretch of beach a couple days later, when an image suddenly appears in my thoughts. I see in my mind's eye, not in reality, a cage on the shore near the water. It is made of metal slats with four-inch open spaces between them. It is about six feet square by eight feet tall, without any obvious door. It is empty.

Very quickly, everything I had described so recently about the Beauty of the scene takes on a new sensation. With the cage there, my curiosity is aroused, and I start making new observations. I think, *Clearly, it has to have been man-made, and somehow it was transported there. A shipwreck? A truck on the beach? It is incongruous with the surroundings. Why a cage and not something else?*

Inside my feelings, I sense the cage as occupying a

hole in the space of the ocean vista. It is such a small object within in the vastness of everything else. I can view it as an unnatural anomaly, harmless of itself. I can even embrace it as still part of the experience of Beauty—as long as it is empty. So I decide to simply accept it being there and continue to enjoy my walk.

Yet … yet there is a subtle, nagging feeling about its symbolism. To cage anything is to take away its freedom; to confine is to limit options. Maybe I should not ignore its message, but I do.

The next day, I walk again along the stretch of seashore. In my imagination, I choose to put some beings inside the cage to explore my own reactions. Outside of it, the Pacific Ocean still stretches to infinity, the waves still crash, the sandpipers still strut. But inside the cage, I imagine

Standing on the Beach, 2016

one seal, one seagull, and one human being. The seal bangs its flipper against the metal, the seagull aimlessly flails into the slats, and the human being sits weeping. My thoughts and feelings go into immediate conflict. Suffering now mars the whole scene of unification. The occupied cage is a site of separation.

I react with new questions: *Are the cage and its contents still part of the connectedness? Is the whole scene not Beautiful now because of the caged beings? Is it ugly just in the space holding the cage?* I observe that when freedom is lost to some, there is a distortion in the space filled with Beauty.

Suddenly, I am in a dilemma. Suddenly, I am in doubt about the Light of Beauty as an all-pervading Source. I sense the contraction I know so well, the contraction of separation. I no longer am sure how to answer the question "Is it Beautiful?"

Separation and Unification

I walk the beach yet again. It is the day after I felt separated from Beauty by my own doubts and confusions. I want to imagine the scene again in search of some understanding of my image of the caged beings on the shore.

I sense my rational mind taking its well-trained scientific approach. I ask *how* questions such as these: *If there is one Light of Beauty always present, how can there be confinement in the midst of freedom or suffering in the midst of joy? How could Beauty seem to come and go to —be present and then not? How can there ever be a "no" answer to the presence of Beauty?*

I wonder if my perspective is distorted by being too close to or too far from what I view. I recall when I thought the whole idea of a view*point* was very limited and should be replaced by a view*space* in which one could see in more dimensions. Perhaps then I could see *how* beautiful and ugly could coexist, *how* they might be actually connected. I want a diagram or a chart or a set of data of probabilities of connections.

I pause and decide that asking *how* questions, though they may lead to some interesting speculation, is the wrong approach for me right now. So I sit awhile on a beached log, my eyes on the ocean waves, and ask different questions,

questions from my heart: *What does my heart feel like when I imagine the prisoners in the cage on the beach? Why is a wordless experience more revealing of the truth?* I can ask no more, for I am overwhelmed with emotional intensity. I start to sob, tentatively hold it back. Inside my head, I scream in agony, *No! No cage! No cage anywhere!*

I feel compassion, abundant compassion, filling my whole body and all the space around me. It is compassion both for myself and for all other living beings. The compassion is connecting me with them! Compassion arose because of cages. It is because of all those cages seen and unseen, cages within myself, cages inside others, cages made by those who mistakenly believe they own what they can confine. I sense one huge sphere of cages scattered across the Earth, holding individuals, groups, any life or what is needed for life! I weep gentle tears of compassion for all of us in such cages, regardless of their size, strength, reason, or time spent.

My rational mind speaks to me with a thought: *Beauty is everywhere connections are freely made. In places where such connections are prevented by confinement, then compassion is required to create the connections. Compassion becomes the Beautiful within those situations that are ugly otherwise. When the answer to "Is it Beautiful?" seems to be "no", one must offer one's gift of compassion before answering.*

I then wonder if being a more aware human means realizing my responsibility to offer compassion whenever or wherever I sense the absence of the Light of Beauty. Such speculations swirl in my head and heart! *Why? Why now?* I wonder if I might be breaking out of one of my own cages right at this very moment. Am I birthing my own liberation as I watch the ocean that birthed life itself?

I breathe. I breathe again. I breathe in the ocean mist and exhale to all. I allow myself to be vulnerable, open. I am less fearful. Something confining me is dissolving away, washing back into the waters.

I don't feel so separated by my own cages any more. Answering the question "Is it Beautiful?" has led me along an evolving pathway to this new awareness of unification with the Light of Beauty. I realize that the process of my human path has always been alternating between separation and unification, but with different intensities and at different times.

These experiences walking on the beach have been teachings for me. I am reminded of a line of my poem "Stuck" from high school: *My feet take turns along the shore between the sand and sea.* I am moving toward an expanded awareness of the unification to which I am already connected. Yet, I doubt I am fully out of my cages. Someday I may ask of myself, "Is it—the human who is *me*—Beautiful?

Chapter 10

REFLECTION 3:
BEAUTY OBSCURED BY ANGER

Shadows of Plants

A Gift of Beauty
(2005)

If you spent a day with me,
walking under the giant sequoia trees,
watching bluebird and fawn and butterfly,
listening to leaves rustling and waterfalls roaring,
would you still?

If you shared with me cheese and an apple
as we exchanged childhood stories,
laughed and cried together sitting by the stream,
would you even then?

If I gave you one day together
filled with the Beauty of Earth and friendship,
would you still ignite the explosives
now tied 'round your waist?

When I experienced the Light of Beauty, her radiance was so intense that no anger could survive in its presence. In the days after, I remember noticing all the anger I had toward my ex-husband, who had divorced me a few years earlier, was simply wiped out. It was as if all the neuronal wiring of my ongoing complaints had just disappeared from my brain. There was no longer anything to forgive or regret. I had been in pain over the loss and had fear about my future. Being angry kept both active. When Beauty extinguished anger, related pain and fear left with it. Beauty had removed a barrier within myself, one that otherwise might have obscured her presence.

Anger *from* Me

I have been angry toward others many times. One of my strongest as an adult was when I first discovered the reality about being a woman in chemistry. I inquired about a summer job in 1963 at a chemical company lab and was told, "We can't hire you because we don't have any 'facilities' [i.e., bathrooms] for women." I was shocked. I was angry at the absurdity and the inequality. It was a motivating anger, an I'll-show-them anger—not in the sense of enacting revenge but of my inner determination to pursue chemistry.

During my professional life in chemistry, I heard many comparable absurdities as I discovered a society openly prejudiced toward women working *outside* their male-approved roles. But I was in total disbelief when my own father said to me in 1980, long after my PhD and initial success in teaching, "With all your education and background, you would make a great wife for a man who is trying to get ahead in his career." My silent reaction was, *Whaaa? What did you just say?* I remember this happening when we were driving back from visiting my mother's gravesite. I wonder if she turned over in it.

I used to hide my anger at others in a secret don't-complain place in my brain, where it could fester rather than heal. I did this with my anger toward the chemistry profession especially. After all, I wanted the job! As described in the autobiography section, when I just couldn't take it anymore, I left what I loved most: teaching organic chemistry. After many years, I ultimately returned to teaching with deeper conviction and stronger courage. It was *after* the Light of Beauty entered my life and I realized no anger should keep me from contributing what I most loved to offer.

Anger *toward* Me

I am human, and some of the mistakes I've made have upset individuals I've known, though never because I was consciously intent on hurting them. I have many times received anger from others. When my pain from it was very deep, it taught me how *anger separates.* Uncontrolled and ongoing anger can sever relationships and destroy mutual trust. It can erect impenetrable walls around itself and harden in its own isolation. Having witnessed what happens to those angry with me has helped me be more objective in order to temper rather than enhance their emotional intensity. I have also learned anger can obscure the Beauty always still present in angry people. Responding to their Beauty rather than their anger is an ideal worth striving for.

Sometimes I'm the one angry with me! Some part of me gets very cross about what another part of me has mistakenly done. I seem to take the role of an authority from my young life, like a parent or a priest. I hear my own inner voice angrily saying what one of them would say. My self-anger separates me from parts of myself. As I have matured, I have learned to heal my old self-anger and lessen, if not transform, any that is new. Realizing that anger obscures my own Beauty and can temporarily separate me from awareness of her is reason enough to make every effort not to become angry in the first place.

Anger *through* Technology

My direct experience with anger from others has been limited primarily to individual people I know. I have never felt like I should be fearful for my physical safety with them. It is a whole different matter when there is an angry group of strangers that might turn to violence, as in a public protest event.

Advanced technology has made easy and instant communication possible around the world. Network access means angry people can find large numbers of other like-minded angry people. It has aided those who want to express and justify their anger and not be held accountable. I'm still holding hope that many such people really do search for a site on anger management or self-compassion instead.

One experience several years before retirement taught me a valuable, though very painful, lesson about group anger from unidentified people. After the UCLA campus-wide network was set up during early 2001, a student-run site was established for comments about professors. The site was deeply flawed in many ways. It was without checkpoints, so anyone who knew me *or not,* anyone who took one of my courses *or not,* anywhere at UCLA *or not,* could anonymously evaluate me as many times as he or she wanted with only obvious profanity edited out. Comments were all public to anyone else, anywhere else. As there were other well-established and fair means of evaluating my teaching, both the department and I had always had student input. It was very clear that the site, even with positive comments, was skewed toward angry responses.

In short, it hurt terribly, really terribly. I was dealing with an invisible, angry group of strangers for the first time. No doubt some were students whom I had turned into the dean for cheating or who had not gotten the grades they wanted. It felt like they were using the site to sabotage my courses. Technology had revealed a new reality that took a piece of my heart out of teaching. I felt shattered, but I kept trying to do my best to sustain my record of excellence … and I cried a lot.

Observing the practice of online trolling today, I could say that my experience fifteen years earlier was trolling in its infancy. Through the network, anger can breed anger now by a feedback intensification process on a global scale. There have not been self-restraints enough to impede the trend, so anger is daring to become an international convention of behavior.

Whatever the online group or purpose, vulnerable people can be drawn into levels of anger way beyond what they might feel normally. The media seem to report news of angry incidents more frequently. Even our vocabulary is expanding to include terms like *road rage* and *gone ballistic.* Brutality also appears to be accelerating as anger moves along its spectrum toward the extreme of violence. It's as if there is an *International Anger and Brutality Competition* in progress and the world is invited.

Excluding major wars, in my own lifetime it seems society has moved far from the anger of a local argument kept private among family members or between street gangs. We are now in an era of anger shared and intensified by groups of dispersed strangers, an anger directed as part of a wide-reaching battle against other strangers for reasons often not even clear. I wonder at times if some people enjoy anger just for the thrill of an emotional arousal that makes them feel alive and noticed. If so, it's a sad indicator of the lack of the healthy interpersonal interactions all humans need to share.

My 1963 anger at not having bathroom facilities for women in a chemistry lab for the purpose of excluding women seems laughable in the context of a 2017 anger held by multitudes across the planet for the purpose of excluding, if not eliminating, other multitudes. Technology has offered a new communication tool for many wondrous things, but it can become a weapon of anger as well. Nonetheless, I still believe no one else's anger should keep any of us from contributing our positive gifts.

Choice: Beauty or Anger?

As I wrote this reflection about anger in my earlier life, I was surprised to find that I got angry! The feeling arose without any obvious specific stimulus. Most likely, it came from distant unpleasant memories being revisited. What concerns me is whether my own threshold to angry arousal has been subliminally influenced by the internet and media reporting.

If our global objective is to move toward a more harmonious, kind humanity, then resolving our disagreements with anger in check is necessary for progress. The shift from anger begins with each of us making choices about how we will respond to anger arising within ourselves or from others. For me, the profound impact of the Light of Beauty serves as my reference experience, so I will speak of unification and separation from that perspective.

When I say one of my basic premises is that *Beauty unites,* I don't mean Beauty creates rigid structures of sameness that cannot change form. I mean unification is a process better called *dynamic, diversified unification.* It is *dynamic* because there is an ongoing making and breaking of connections to create new forms as the expansion of universal Beauty naturally evolves. It is *diversified* because it unites existing diverse forms into new diverse forms. Consider, for example, that the diverse atoms within stars ultimately connected into human beings. There is an overall arc of transformation from one simpler state of unification to a more highly complex one. Because of our consciousness, humans can experience states of thought and emotions that are diverse within and among ourselves. I see Beauty guiding us on a new arc of transformation. *It is an arc that disconnects our diverse reasons for fighting and unifies us through reconnection of new, diverse reasons for not fighting.*

As mentioned previously, another basic premise of mine is that *anger separates.* The nature of my anger seems to be to get rid of something, push it away, destroy it, separate from it. *You hurt my feelings, so get away from me. You are on my land, so get off of it.* In the psychological development of a child, there is a need for separation as part of identifying a *me* for the first time. A child's response to perceived invasion of identity might be displays of anger and aggression over what is *mine!* The important question is whether a child transitions into an adult who also has empathy toward others and understands the value of constraining anger for healthy relationships. If we accept the Beauty within ourselves, it becomes easier to feel empathy for others. If we learn that anger separates us from Beauty, we may be able to view anger in others without participating in it.

When I experience from my deepest heart what happens between anger and Beauty, it is a sensation without words. Yet I am driven to allow words to flow as a metaphor of what I am experiencing. I do so below.

A Vision of Anger and Beauty

I stand on a flat surface in a void. I slowly turn my head to see an angry person some distance away. The reason for the anger is of no interest, only the anger's presence. I imagine it emanating as a dark vapor from the pores of the person's whole body. The anger swirls completely around the person to form a tight protective cover. The person becomes a dark human pillar of anger.

I know somehow I will choke on the anger if I do not keep separated.

I turn my head back, only to find others also standing, each hidden by his or her own dark vapor—the darker, the angrier. There are so many! They stand everywhere I look, all around me, even into the horizon! They are separated from each other by emptiness. Some are gathered in groups, small or large, with so much combined anger it spreads as an outer layer encasing the group solidly as one.

Without warning, all the pillars start to move at once, different directions, different speeds. They seem to multiply. I become alarmed they'll come my way and I will be suffocated. Where can I go? What can I do? I must, absolutely must, be able to breathe free of them.

I am urgently seeking refuge when I suddenly become aware of another presence that had been obscured. It first appears as dim, small balls of light in the spaces between the pillars. Then the balls brighten everywhere at once, a single entity of Light. The pillars of anger are unknowingly submerged in it, their own darkness obscuring their ability to see outwardly. The Light is the Light of Beauty, and it offers me a familiar safety as I move calmly into its radiance.

But I am not alone there. I find other people. There is no anger in them, no dark vapor obscuring them. All are emitting continuous light from their own hearts. They form a multitude of hearts without anger. I sense they are ready ... ready ... but for what, I don't know.

I wait ... in hope, in faith ... I wait.

Then it begins. It starts as a small motion seemingly from nowhere. My eyes closed, I feel it against my skin, a soft breeze from all directions. It stirs a deep longing within myself for unification. I want to exhale forgiveness out of my heart. As I begin to do so, I realize I am one of many without anger. We are all releasing the Light of Beauty from our hearts to create a breeze of forgiveness. It moves into the spaces between the pillars of anger and slowly disperses their dark vapor with its gentle touch. At first only a little here, a little there. The anger weakens its hold. The obscurity preventing them from seeing and being seen lifts as the dark vapor is slowly transformed into translucent emptiness filled with Light.

It is overwhelming: so many hearts without anger, so generous, offering their Light to free those who cannot free themselves. Our community of radiant wind is scented with forgiveness. At this, I can answer yes to the question, "Is it Beautiful?"

Return to Reality

I awaken, however, still in a reality where anger travels on the data of tweets, sits in the cars of traffic jams, stones other humans, tortures other animals, kills innocent children, enjoys bigotry, and more. It is the presence of such anger that stirs difficult questions: *Is it enough for me to simply believe every human has Beauty within, however dim the light at times, and that anger can obscure but not annihilate Beauty's presence there? Am I committed enough to release the wind of forgiveness from my own heart to blow away their defensive vapor? How can I transform my thoughts and images into meaningful actions?*

For it comes down to what each one of us decides to do in any one moment. Right *now,* will I neutralize the anger within myself or express it without restraint? Right *now,* will I risk reprisals by speaking out calmly against those who would foment anger? Right *now,* will I offer even-tempered alternatives to angry interactions? The opportunities for actions to decrease levels of anger will be available to me. Within those moments, what will I decide to *do*?

These decisions are the difficult reality that must be addressed as it arises. Yet we need not wait to imagine the future reality we long for. I imagine each of us overcoming the anger nearest us, including our own. I imagine us as a *we* guiding humanity away from anger and toward participation in the evolutionary process of unification. I imagine us empowered by Beauty to move with her along the arc of humanity's next transformation.

I long for a day I may not see in my lifetime, the day humanity becomes a harmonious chorus singing in full voice, *"Yes!"* in answer to our common question, "Are *we* Beautiful?"

* * *

Related Poem

Below is a poem that was written over ten years ago when it seemed everywhere I looked, I saw an attitude of "It's *your* fault!" The media was lit up with fingers pointing blame at someone and stories of someone suing someone. I was concerned at that time about what kind of society we were becoming. Although I have no specific data, when blame started to be the lead news topic, it seemed to spread like a virus. I wondered about greed-driven lawsuits. I wondered about taking responsibility for our actions. It saddened me and created anxiety within me lest I make even an innocent mistake. Blame stills goes on, but now the front-page behavioral topic is fueled by anger.

So I wonder, *Is indiscriminate blame the first step toward indiscriminate anger? Have we become an indiscriminate society—that is, one not concerned with exercising careful judgment?*

The Sadness of Blame
(2006)

Where there is injustice, disaster, criminality, or disease,
someone suffers—body, mind, spirit.
It is within the Nature of our world and our humanity
for the paths of forces to intercept,
whether meteorite to city or brick to shoe,
whether stray bullet to a passerby's heart
or ignorance to sensitivity.
There is sadness for those who suffer
from such uninvited events.

I have cried for trees lost to forest fires,
homes lost to mudslides,
cities lost to tsunamis, libraries lost to bombings,
races lost to genocide, children lost to starvation.
Will there never be an end to these tears
streaming from the experience of suffering
that connects us all.

For some, tears are the last resort after rage.
With a perception of immanent death,
their fear may birth anger
to fuel defense against the invisible
or to disguise a pain too intense to bear.
Yet after such primal blindness passes,
their eyes are freed to release a watery grief
and healing may begin.

Others blame.

With the evolution of human reason
we have been endowed with tools to alleviate suffering:
knowledge leading to prevention,
understanding leading to remedies,
communication leading to mediation.
But still we revert to blame,

a behavior not observed in the
rivers, plants, and animals.
It is an invention of mankind,
perhaps intended to stabilize societies
by recognizing responsibility for our actions.
We have taken that simple need for community
and created complex laws to define, in minute detail,
intent and fault and harm.

Our children learn to practice on siblings
rather than accept correction for their own misdeeds.
We have confused serving justice
with earning a badge of entitlement or source of income.
We hunt for another to blame or make suffer as well,
whether for the most heinous acts
or for the most trivial of human errors.
Blaming is the new weapon of our times,
made more treacherous by its invisibility,
allowing us to grant millions for the spilling of hot coffee
rather than spend it on victims
of devastating earthquakes.

The logic of identifying responsibility for actions
and making detached corrections to restore balance
has been overtaken by the desire for revenge
or the opportunity for a talk-show appearance.
So we repeat our painful stories,
distort them in our reenactments,
wag our fingers in blame,
and create mental lockboxes
to keep every pain ever present
lest the justification for our behavior be diminished,
lest we accept our own responsibility to release.

The sadness of blame is that the suffering remains,
ignored and unattended and hidden within,
waiting endlessly to dissolve through forgiveness,

never freed to heal,
unable to soften the heart,
powerless to create a peaceful solution,
thus leaving the ones who blame
abandoned in their own prisons of misguided desires.

So my tears flow not only for those who suffer
by uninvited criminality, disaster, or disease,
but also for those who choose to blame,
unaware that their self-invited affliction
is the deeper sadness.

* * *

Second Related Poem

Around the same time and closely related to my thoughts about blame, I was overwhelmed with a sense of deep, deep sadness. It almost felt as if I were Earth herself carrying too much mass on her surface. I believe this was due in large part to the wars in the Middle East still going on. I sensed I represented all the misguided or confused values and behaviors of so many people. The following poem helped sort out my awareness and feelings.

The Great Sadness
(2006)

I feel the Great Sadness
from images of war in distant places
brought home by satellite,
the blood and wounds and draped bodies
shrunken on the screen
to lessen the intensity of the reality

that someone made a choice to kill.

What is it one must hide
that reasons are invented to disguise assault?
Is it an addiction to power,
an avoidance of the effort of self-inquiry,
a heart disconnected from the Divine,
or simple idiocy?

Perhaps those who chose to fight
cannot see the complexity of the human landscape,
have no interest in learning the interplays
of intellect and culture and emotion and history,
take no enjoyment in the variations of experiences
within the commonality of our humanness,
or do not care to recognize
our multi-dimensional interweaving.

Why would anyone even try
to eliminate his/her own inadequacies
by demolishing the finest gifts of others:
attacking ideas of the intellectually evolved,
who have initiatives for creative solutions,
or attacking good deeds of the compassionate,
who inspire by service in generosity,
or attacking global values of the wise ones,
who strive to express our unifying principles.
They seem to believe, these choosers of death,
that they have the authority to starve in others
what they do not know how to nurture in themselves.
In their defiance of differences from their beliefs,
in their demands for unchallenged obedience,
and in their decrees of performances
validating their righteousness,
they slay by bloodless deteriorations
so leisurely as to be superficially invisible in the moment.

And so the Great Sadness comes over me
that they cannot see the Beauty of the living fabric
cloaking Earth with its diversity of patterns.
They have not learned
that to empower others to lift themselves
expands the consciousness of the planet.
They do not know how to practice the art
of subtle communications
through the fields of the heart
in harmony with the intellect.
And saddest of all, by not knowing what they don't know,
they continue to choose to kill.

Each time someone re-enacts this violence
in miniature form
by assaulting some aspect of my own self,
I am reminded of his/her companions across the lands.
I first feel the direct sting to my own heart,
revisit the emotional history of my personal pains,
then weep in the Great Sadness
for all the hearts so empty as my attacker's.
Perhaps the small, imperceptible wound inflicted on me
with a word or a look or a gesture or a slap
serves to revive a napping awareness within myself
of the need for my contribution to universal compassion
through my response to the assassin nearest me.

For it is, after all, just this:
the inflictor has yet to sense his own affliction.

Chapter 11

REFLECTION 4: BEAUTY AND JOY

Perhaps Joy is something we experience
on its way through us
to someone else.

At my country home, the most scenic view is on the side facing the high mountains, valley, and river. One day, I was walking outside along the opposite side of the house, which faces lower nearby hills. I had gotten up very early to do some chores. It was semi-dark. As I came around the corner of the house to face the scenic side, I looked, stopped immediately in my tracks, and gasped out loud. I just stood there as if transported to some alien planet. No, it wasn't a local rattlesnake—at least, not that time. It was the light of the sunrise, and it was stunning!

As the sun had not fully risen over the closest mountain across the valley, light spread instead around its edges to make patterns on surfaces in its path. Trees and rocks bathed in an orange glow cast elongated shadows. Other light reflected off or passed through scattered clouds. There were magnificent pastels in shades of pink and red that merged into brilliant white rays of light from the sun's still-hidden origin behind the mountain. The lit clouds reflected their colored patterns off the surface of the river below; colors rippled with the river's flow in contrast to its shaded surroundings. The Beauty was immense! It covered an open view of more than half the sky! All thoughts in my mind stopped as I was completely overcome with awe. Beauty wrapped her arms around it all, with me, a speck in the wholeness of the scene, a single human creature consciously observing her. I stood in her embrace as the progression of changes of colors and lit surfaces kept pace with Earth's slow rotation toward the sun.

What I first felt when I came around the side of the house was intense joy! In retrospect, I might describe it as a "Kosmic Peekaboo" moment! The scene was hidden until I passed the corner; then it was instantly there. I suppose my reaction was much like that of an infant when a mother hides her face behind a barrier. There's a moment of sheer delight when the familiar face suddenly reappears. I gasped instead of giggling, but I have no doubt joy was traveling throughout my body. Needless to say, I forgot about my chores. I lingered instead with the feeling of Beauty's presence.

I lingered in curiosity as well. I wondered, *What is the relationship of Beauty and Joy?*

The Expression of Joy

Joy elicits a sense of pleasure but, like most emotions, covers a range of intensities with corresponding descriptive words. For me, joy might be a simple *delight* (example, a chocolate cookie), *euphoria* (example, an operatic aria), or

113

something between, such as *exhilaration* (example, giving a chemistry lecture—for me, anyway!).

When I imagine an exceptionally joyful person, I see someone with arms opened wide, to the side or as a V above the head. The person's chest may be a bit out or the head back. Always there's a smile, and the person may even jump. Body postures that expose the heart and throat signal a release from constraints of fear of attack at these vulnerable sites. Arms up and outstretched signal the person feels free to expand into the surrounding space. On other occasions, a person may simply express joy by a broad smile, perhaps also with head tilted. Our body language communicates to others the joy we are experiencing and also teaches us something about the nature of true joy: a heart feeling more expansive, a willingness to expose vulnerabilities, a sense of liberation.

I believe it's true that *joy evokes joy.* One person's expressed joy can be experienced empathically within another. When there is a group interaction, one joyful person can encourage joy to spread within the group. In short, expressing joy can connect us.

Why *Not* Joy?

There are moments when propriety takes precedence over expressing joy—for example, consoling someone who has just lost a loved one. There are also moments when our own physical or emotional pain is so severe that it dominates our senses and inhibits joy. If I assume joy can be *chosen,* a joy to enhance our experience of being alive, then what reasons might prevent us from choosing such joy?

I reflected on this question as I walked with my dog on a nature trail one early autumn morning. I asked myself at one point, *Do I feel joy right now?* My answer was that I felt *neutral.* I was analyzing joy with my thoughts. I wasn't feeling it or anything else identifiable. I decided to be more attentive to what might bring me joy in that moment. Still walking, I observed beautiful scenes around me, wondered if my dog was joyful when he sniffed the ground, and noted many positive events in my current life. Yet I felt a resistance to experiencing a feeling of joy, as if something were obscuring my access. I wondered, *Why?*

I was surprised when the memory of an old voice answered, *You are not worthy.* Well, *that* was a quick reminder that my indoctrination of being born with original sin still remains deep in my neuronal wiring! I asked myself, *Is joy something one has to earn? Am I only allowed to be joyful when I've done my duties first?* I may have learned some version of these falsehoods in my distant past, but now I can override them by choosing joy as I live. I don't believe I am denied access to joy or need a *good behavior* note from some outside authority to experience it. However, I may need to forgive myself for any human errors now and then.

Accessing Joy

As I continued walking, I chose to accept joy in those moments, for no other reason than because it was available and brought pleasure to my sense of being. I was surprised, nonetheless, that it took what felt like a decisive *push* from within my heart to connect to joy. Like an unclogged drain, joy then flowed quickly into my awareness as a physical rush of intense happiness. During those brief moments, I only felt flows of joyful energy within my being.

Then I asked myself, *What just happened?* It seemed there was a stepwise process. My heart was touched by something first, and only then opened to joy. I wondered if the Light of Beauty emanating from my surroundings first touched my heart and then the Light opened a pathway or conduit for Universal Joy. Or maybe Beauty distracted me from my resistance long enough for joy to find entry through my heart.

There are many ways to access joy. Sometimes when I connect to joy, it's a reflex action. Something very special has surprised me and my urge is to throw my arms in the air, smile broadly, and say aloud, *"Wow!"* On such occasions, I don't consciously seek joy—it just reveals itself to me. On other occasions, I am aware of the presence of joy in small ways, and my response may be a simple smile and sense of contentment. I wondered, *Do I have to wait for joy to flow into my awareness? It seems I can also intentionally seek her out at any time.* Certainly in ordinary moments, like washing the dishes or filling the car with gas, I can choose to be joyful about it and maybe even smile.

Being Joyful

I had thought writing about joy would be a joyful activity. After all, I've had so many joyful moments during my own life and was well acquainted with the feeling. Yet something beyond my presumed *unworthiness* kept me unsettled about the topic. I had a nagging sense that I was not realizing something very important—or maybe many things.

For example, joy and misery coexist on Earth. Sometimes I feel it is *improper* for me to experience my own joy knowing there is so much misery elsewhere. Even this very day, I saw horrible photos of drowned refugees on a boat from Libya. I have a very difficult time experiencing joy while my heart carries such painful images. I do know my moments of joy do not replace my compassion for others who are simultaneously suffering. I also believe generosity is exceptionally important. Through generous giving to those in need, we connect to them, ease their suffering, *and* feel joyful doing so.

I know there are some joys I especially value and express. For example, I value joyful times with friends, joy from teaching, joy from creative writing, joy from holding a door open for someone at a store, and much more. Some so-called "joys" I consider questionable. Most notable is the joy of acquiring *things*. In our culture, we are barraged with ads showing happy people who have acquired *stuff*. The message is that to be joyful, we must consume goods. I have fallen for this many times, only to find myself possessed by my possessions. It is true there is a sense of pleasure associated with the *novelty* of new things, but it is easy to be lured into cages of banal materialism. If we do so, we risk losing our ability to discriminate between what is and isn't meaningful joy.

Universal Joy

I keep wondering about my sense of a much bigger context including joy and misery that also involves the role of Beauty. Perhaps there is another perspective of joy, one more difficult to put into words because it is experienced in a realm without words. Yet I must use words here and will do so with imagery in the following vision.

A Vision of Joy

I float weightless like a human satellite above Earth. Below, I see a cloudless planet completely covered with a mantle of semitransparent blue light reaching all the way up to me. The light is bluer in some regions than others, and there are occasional open gaps through which Earth's surface is clearly visible.

I gaze in fascination—until I unexpectedly zoom onto Earth's surface. I am in a house where a baby has just been born. No one sees me. I watch a family smile at the baby and each other. Other children are singing and dancing gleefully. There are presents by the bed and candles burning. The whole room is filled with the same semitransparent blue light. I know it is joy being created due to the birth of the baby.

An abundant wave of that joy suddenly carries me out of the room. I laugh as I bounce along its undulations. I then realize the blue light surrounding Earth is Universal Joy. I unite with it and travel until we reach an open gap. There is such an abundance of Universal Joy that it easily flows over the edge of the gap like a gentle waterfall, carrying me downward with it. When I land on Earth, I rebound repeatedly until I settle unhurt among rubble. There is no blue light there, only the remains from an earthquake—and the sound of a woman screaming.

In anguish, she yells, "Save my child! Please, someone save my child!" I see the waterfall of blue light begin to move in her direction, as if in response to her call. As it approaches, it safely pushes a group of neighbors who are hurrying to her aid. It provides strength to them as they clear the rubble. The child is found alive, and the blue light engulfs them all. The presence of Universal Joy is there.

Was the local joy of the child just born sent through Universal Joy to save another child from misery?

I zoom high above again and watch the flows of Joy moving in its mantle around Earth. In some regions, Joy flows up from the surface of Earth into the mantle. In other regions, Joy flows down into the gaps. And I understand a new meaning. Local joy connects to Universal Joy, which amplifies, freely travels to where needed or requested or sent, gives strength to those vulnerable, enables them to smile, and liberates them from misery. As Joy connects, so do people.

Unification

I am reminded of what has always brought me my deepest joys, namely *connections*—connections to Nature, to friends, to fulfilling work, to ideas, to those I offer acts of kindness or generosity, and especially connections to Beauty. All joyful connections are moving me toward a state of unification. Perhaps herein lies the relationship of Beauty and Joy.

I believe the Light of Beauty has guided me on a pathway of understanding and experiencing Universal Joy. Beauty has lifted obscurity hiding Joy's eternal presence by easing the release of my sense of unworthiness. She has reminded me of my many generous offerings to others throughout my life and the joys I have known through them. Beauty has offered me an abundance of joy from

Nature. Beauty nudges me when materialistic intrusions try to lure me away from the deeper meaning of true Joy.

If I were to ask, "Is *my* Joy Beautiful?", my answer would be yes because, for me, true Joy does not exist without Beauty. Universal Joy is an inseparable attribute of the Light of Beauty.

No matter where each of us humans literally is at this very moment, we can choose to connect through our common Universal Joy. An exchange of smiles among us connects our simple actions done joyfully. Spreading our arms in a V demonstrates our sharing of expansive, liberating joy. Through our intentions in meditation or prayer, we can send our joy into the gaps of suffering around Earth. We can share a grander part of our humanity with each other and with Earth herself through the sharing of Universal Joy.

I see my own joy as a gift to Universal Joy to be distributed to those in need, whoever and wherever they are. I see my joy as a part of a pattern of connections of all humans. I have often heard it said, and have felt it true, that humans who have suffered understand and connect more deeply to other humans who also have. I would suggest that humans who have known great joy could also understand and connect more deeply to other humans who have. Perhaps both are true simply because we connect better to those with shared experiences. In these uncertain times of worldwide transitions into a new era of existence on Earth, I would encourage us all to give more attention and intention to sharing Universal Joy.

I long for the day when we ask together, "Is *our* Joy

Beautiful?" I long to hear the answer from all of humanity
as a coordinated jump of *"Yes!"* vibrating around the world.

* * *

Moment of Joy
(2013)

Sun setting
shadows on the trail
wildflowers displaying
their sleepy rays of Beauty
while my dog smells
the same ground as yesterday
as if his purpose
is to update the story
of his path.

Walking just us two
I am free
to raise my arms
skip my step
hum or sing my tune
allow my body
the motions of joy
without the sense of it
as if to call forth joy
in reverse of a joy felt
before its expression.

And so did joy answer
my opened arms
and song of invitation
and join me in those moments
teaching me it is always there
waiting for me

to will it into my awareness
with voice or dance
or maybe someday
simply by acceptance.

* * *

Though not specifically written with the intent of
focusing on joy, this poem captures for me some of the
sensations and reflections of joy.

Extension
(2005)

I stretch my arms to the stars
extend them fervently
into the dark night
palms open, fingers spread
I swirl my V into a cone
that stars may pour into my heart
or I may spray my heart out to them.

I try to will myself elastic,
become a rubber band of flesh,
to extend beyond my planet of experiences
and touch the mothers of my matter.
All the while the stars' faint glow
extends as well across the space between
and channels its light touch
into my longing.

I want to lift away,
rise above in space or ahead in time,
or beyond them both,
but I forget

extension is in two directions
plus and minus, light and dark,
sky and soil, past and future,
so I go deep to nourish
my flight to the heavens
only to realize on the way
that I am always extended into both
from the point of *Who I Am.*

PART III

TOWARD UNIFICATION

Separation and Unification

The Passerby
(2005)

She asked a passerby the way
and he but looked as if to say,
"There, each road is what you seek.
Only listen to the sounds of feet
to hear how they trod, heavy or light,
then you will know a truth, not fright.
All paths upon a sphere will lead
you home again and you will see,
the nature of the walk was all."

Toward Unification

If asked, "Where is your life's pathway going now?", I would not hesitate to answer, "I'm returning home."

It is not the home of a rental apartment or house, not the sheltering security of a job or money, not even the covering of meaningful relationships. The *home* I'm going toward now is the Oneness of Existence from which I was born. I came into life using preexisting matter and energy reorganized to create my human body. I have evolved to a mature person as I have lived my experiences in relationship with Earth and its inhabitants. My constant fundamental attribute along the way has been that *I exist.* For the most part, I have identified my *self* by my story of sequential events. That story still has a significant chapter to be written. I suspect it will be about Beauty and service and little about my *self.* Perhaps the *self* of my stories will shrink as my awareness of the Oneness of my being expands its boundaries into the space remaining.

Reviewing some aspects of my past story at this point

126

will draw attention to especially significant moments. First, I offer a poem to introduce the flow I experienced before writing what follows.

Within and Without
(2016)

Existence within me, existence without,
I entered Earth undefined as one with Oneness
with instructions in coded atoms
to divide, separate, become diverse,
to exist among others,
among paradoxes, confusions, ambiguities
with one deep longing: *return home.*

Gifted as a human with self-awareness,
itself the cause and answer to limitations,
life continued within me
as outdated beliefs disconnected themselves
and new connections reached for higher dimensions.
Evolution did not pass me by,
did not leave my longing untouched
but ignited by a new gift of Light.

Beauty illuminated hidden meanings
of reunion through Truth exposed
if I dared to discern expansion and contraction
of my thoughts, my heart, my both
in rhythm with a beatless Oneness
of existence within me, existence without.

I am ready to strip my selfness bare
look directly into the Light of Beauty,
without polarized lenses permitting illusions,
that I might see her formless origins
of all I hold dear expressed in forms,

> hear her invitation of service
> to the incomprehensible Oneness
> of which I am a participant.
> For existence without me
> will continue when I release it within.

Very early as a child, I separated how I experienced life into two pathways. Simply put, I could call them science and spirit, but it is more complex than that. I might say logic and feeling, rationality and intuition, materiality and immateriality, words and wordlessness, or intellect and heart. Whatever the choice of words, I have traveled these two pathways all my life. I have witnessed the value of each within their respective contexts. I have honored them as two pathways of human knowledge of existence. Both have stirred my curiosity and provided answers—one to questions of "How does it all work?", the other to questions of "What does it all mean?" The answers have never really been adequate alone, but have begged me for integration.

My experience with the Light of Beauty was the most profound of my life. It challenged all my previous conceptions of both paths of knowledge. It seemed to have downloaded awareness too expansive for me to grasp all at once and so has trickled out its experiential significance over the years. Beauty has been a presence treasured, a presence at times seemingly lost, a presence serving as a dilemma to resolve, and most importantly, a connection to that which is way beyond my individual self.

I have been most aware of Beauty when I have been in natural settings away from cities and crowds of people. I have found her in the deep woods, by the sides of mountain streams, in the crashing of ocean waves on the shore, in the eyes of my dog, in moments under skies so dark every star in the Milky Way seemed within reach. In those moments, my path of science was silenced by the realization that how it *all* worked was beyond my capacity to know. Feeling so connected to Beauty when surrounded by Nature is no doubt what led me to purchase acreage in the foothills where I now live. Retiring to this small village felt like *coming home.* As I walk by the large picture windows in my home, Nature-friends are always in sight: trees, animals, mountains, rocks, river, sky, clouds, and stars. I have had the very great gift of human friends in our village with whom to share this appreciation and our lives here.

Without the demands of teaching organic chemistry dominating my days, I have been able to pursue other areas of science on my own. I have not given up my enjoyment of and curiosity about studying fields of research new to me. My favorites have been cosmology and neuroscience—the cosmos birthed all the matter and laws of existence that led to the evolution of a human brain able to consciously explore itself. Questions of *how it works* for both of these fields of exploration push me, as they did in chemistry, to an edge where the next obvious question is "What does it all mean?" I have viewed the chemistry of my past as training for rational thinking and as a means of appreciation for the complex Beauty of scientific knowledge in general.

Having affirmed my pathway of scientific interconnections, I felt I could focus on a deeper spiritual relationship with Beauty as my next phase of unification. At one point, I tried to make a list of attributes of Beauty to guide me to decide whether something is, in fact, Beautiful. This approach might seem normal if one were doing a science experiment—much like defining an insect by how many legs, what kind of skeleton, etc. I came to my senses quickly, however, and decided such a list was the wrong approach entirely for recognizing Beauty. Using such an approach assumes Beauty is a fixed quality defined by external comparisons based on past information. The Beauty of which I speak is to be known by an internal, wordless experience in the present moment.

Here is what I am exploring about Beauty now and why the question "Is it Beautiful?" helps me unify the knowing.

When I wrote the reflections in the middle section of this book, I began to see a pattern emerging. I don't consider Beauty an emotion of itself, but rather I experience it as evoking emotions. In the reflections at the seashore, Beauty led me to deep compassion for those suffering from lack of freedom; in the reflection on anger, Beauty led me to forgiveness of those whose anger obscured their Beauty; in the reflection on joy, Beauty led me to understand joy in relation to misery. After writing these reflections, I felt as if I were viewing them all from a universal viewspace so I could discover their common interconnections. One connection is fundamental within these examples, namely human beings connecting to each other.

What I envisioned was Beauty as an all-encompassing presence of radiance, like an infinite whiteness, visible only in another dimension. Out of it morphed energy shapes representing the Essences of Compassion, Forgiveness, Joy, and many other values for expressing the full potential of human beings. I feel certain Kindness, Patience, and

Generosity are among the many that dwell there. Beauty was the conduit to lead me where these Absolute Essences were created, are sustained, and are made accessible. My first reaction was to wonder: *When I sense something is Beautiful, am I sensing a portal to her reality where I can embody her expressions? Each time I experience Beauty's realm, do I evolve further into my fullest potential in service to the Kosmos?* After all, the summation of all glimpses of Beauty must ultimately coalesce into a vision of the Whole beyond limited human expression. The Whole is called by some *Love* or *God.*

Long ago, I retreated from Beauty's invitation to fully merge with her radiance. Perhaps since then I have been *awakening into Beauty* one small step at a time. It's as if I am slowly moving toward total unification with her Presence, shedding obscurities along the way. Or maybe I have always been a vessel of her Light and am slowly shedding the vessel.

A few years ago, I had a surprise experience during a silent retreat. I was walking along a nearby trail feeling lonely and confused. I pleaded from my heart, *Light of Beauty, where are you?* Simultaneously, the answer in my mind was "Inside you" and I envisioned and physically felt her Light flowing throughout my body. I immediately teared up in gratitude for her Presence. As quickly, I found myself in doubt and wondered if my imagination was playing tricks on me. Yet that momentary *experience* remains vividly in my memory, and I have wondered if there is, in fact, a *Light Body*—or perhaps a *Beauty Body*—available all the time *within* me.

Sometimes more recently, I try to visualize myself

as that *Light Body.* To do so, I must release barriers of fear and mindless chatter. When I have been able to experience my body as a connection of connections that, taken together, identify one human being, I sense myself as one *presence* harmonious within Kosmic Existence in that moment. I want to easily choose that state of presence even when I must use my thoughts to manage myself in the material world.

My curiosity bursts with questions when I reflect on these mysteries. I have said before that I have answers and only need to ask the right questions to recognize them. I must have many answers to have so many questions to ask! But I have found a new set of essential spiritual questions, such as, *Who am I without a "self"? How do I serve a Oneness that would seem by definition to already have everything within it*? Disconnecting and reconnecting anew as I transition to new states of awareness seems a natural personal evolution. *In short, the form I call my "self" is in an ongoing natural process of discovering experiences beyond my limited "self-ness."*

I will continue to share future experiences, those on the boundary between wordless reality and mental images that could be translated into words. These experiences seem to come in and out of existence somewhat randomly but with a hint of deeper meaning. Perhaps they are trying to blossom from within the radiance of Beauty and await a more expansive opening of my heart to be released.

I must admit there is some fear of the inner changes I am certain are coming. I am advised that fear of the future means I am not present in this moment. Yet, in this present moment, I have decisions to make that will impact how I handle the future. I believe identifying my fears can help remove them as obstructions. This is when my intellect serves as a partner to help my spirit reveal itself. I continue to address the experience of fear, as in this recent poem.

The Life of Fear
(2017)

Heat of volcano
teeth of lion
venom of snake
prion of beef
killers all
penetrating defenses
of the living.

Innate responses
programmed countermeasures
matter duels with matter
as nature evolves its own life
in reflex survival of identity
formed *without fear.*

~~~

Measurement by humans:
fault-break of Earth
MRI of brain
balance of checkbook
count of bodies
code of gene.

Conscious intelligence
operates with reflex
to imagination
not to certainty,

133

numbers, probabilities
expand options of futures,
excite thoughts
of needless neurons
firing to nowhere
but distraction,
concoct states
unreal in the moment
to *birth fears.*

~~~

Human self-awareness
human self-preservation
human self-dependence
veil truth
of human non-self
as one mind tricks another
one thought distorts another
and *fears proliferate.*

~~~

Reality awaits discovery
of its existence
expressed in forms
expressed in processes
all connected as One,
a space already
always,
already
every
where *fear expires*
into emptiness.

I wonder if the future will include changes in my
personal relationships, a shrinking of my possessions,

a revised definition of deep values, a perceptual shift of my *self,* and greater vulnerability. Many adaptations may be required, doubts overcome, judgments questioned, discernment exercised, and spiritual courage invoked. I do not know how I will wander through my own remaining darkness as well as that of others to expose the shared space connecting us. Yet I fear one thing more than any of these: *not* giving the gifts created through me. I am *impelled* to give to others as my expression of gratitude for realizing, if only in part, my own liberation. I want to be open about my own spiritual evolution in hope of encouraging others to be open with theirs.

I see myself offering this gift based on a common process: *creativity.* I believe that to create using one's talents is to participate in the inherent flow of the Kosmos.

The Creative Realm
(c. 2008)

To enter the Creative Realm,
you must leave behind everything.
Otherwise, when you exit,
you will have nothing.

If you do not enter empty, you will not enter completely
and will risk returning with your preconceptions
simply dressed up in new distortions.
To enter empty demands we release our hold
on what holds us.
We must release our misguided beliefs
that we possess anything or control anything.
To enter empty demands we must disconnect
from our pretense of security

135

and interrupt the continuity of our memories
projecting into our future.
Above all, to enter empty demands
we detach ourselves from fear.

We enter not by passing through a portal
but by allowing ourselves to become the portal.
The experience of the Creative Realm is a state of being
that permits restructuring of formless,
unidentified energies
into new probabilities of configurations,
not simply for novelty,
but for Truth.

When we exit the Realm, our state of being
must necessarily contract to our limitations.
We return with a responsibility
to use skills unique to ourselves
to manifest new patterns of connectivity,
for until we choose to enact our expression of the Truth,
it will remain a secret even to ourselves.
So we must paint a new painting, mold a new sculpture,
reason a new theory, take a new measurement,
make a new machine, compose a new melody,
write a new poem, dance a new dance,
relate a new response, speak a new heart.

In this way, no matter how long our visit,
the depth of the Truth,
or the complexity of our expression of its form,
we join others who have also returned
from the Creative Realm.
Together, we participate in a grand weaving of the great
mysteries that accelerate the transformation of us all.

My own participation in the creative realm will no

doubt include words. My goal is to find words to express the wordless experiences of being human. Maybe they will be words to suggest that someone be open to new possibilities or words to sharpen awareness of natural states currently hidden by mindless distractions. I want them to be words of kindness, humility, generosity, and realization of what is already present and unrecognized within us.

Ultimately, I want us all to share what is spiritually meaningful to ourselves individually so we can identify our common values. I believe from our authentically shared diversities, a hopeful new direction for humanity will emerge—one beyond our current imaginations. It seems the natural way to align with universal evolution and reach our highest potential as a species on Earth.

I speak of moving from separation *toward* unification as if one never really gets there. I honestly don't know, as I'm still in motion. Maybe I am simply trying to realize the Light I already am. At times, I feel I am transitioning to a state of complete emptiness that is beyond all my questions, a state where one answer has always been and there is nothing left to ask. I once, long, long ago, wrote:

> *I long for the day*
> *I have no need to say*
> *these words.*

In the meantime, I still need words.

My personal history expressed through this work has reached a point where my main focus is shifting to *return home* along the pathway of Beauty. I retain my secondary pathway of knowledge through science to support rational discernment needed as long as I am in my bodily form. Still, it is Beauty who provides spiritual clarity and strength as I move forward. I wonder if at some point in writing this book, it was no longer me doing the writing, but Beauty herself. Or maybe that is to come. I wonder if these words are intended for all of us and I am already becoming her willing conduit as I learn what it means to be a human who is *being*.

> *I don't know, I don't know*
> *as the urge to know wanes*
> *and the longing for Beauty remains.*

My most basic guiding question has become "Is it Beautiful?" It is a question that I can ask of my thoughts, my heart, my choices, or anything that may present itself for my embrace. It is a question that enlarges my viewspace of context, liberates me from past cages, focuses me as observer of the present moment, and brings peace. When I ask it, I am acknowledging my longing to bring forth Beauty's presence in service to all of us.

So if I were to ask right now, "Is *my pathway* Beautiful?", I believe Beauty's voice from throughout the Kosmos would gently whisper her answer to me, in harmony with all existence, this single word:

Yes!

* * *

Oneness Waiting
(c. 2005)

I am the Sight of Oneness.
Look for me.
I can be seen within the mysteries
of your mind and heart
and outside them both.
I am the vision between matter and energy
and I am their connector.
I am available in the timeless space of Now
only to be seen by you.
When will you choose to look?
I am the Sight of Oneness, waiting.

I am the Voice of Oneness.
Listen for me.
I can be heard over the rhythms of your heart
and under the cacophony of your surroundings.
I am the silence between words and breath
and I am their sound.
I am an ever-present messenger
from the Oneness.
I am available in the timeless space of Now
only to be heard by you.
When will you choose to listen?
I am the Voice of Oneness, waiting.

I am the Joy of the Oneness, always present.
I am the Innocence of Oneness, always present.
I am the Intimacy of the Oneness, always present.
I am the Beauty of Oneness, always present.
When will you choose to smile with me,
play with me, accept my ready kiss,
experience my light?
I am the One of Oneness, waiting.

APPENDICES

Appendices

A. Luceigh Bio

B. Index of Book Poems

C. Guided Visualization and Teaching:
Beauty in the Green Valley

Appendix A

LUCEIGH BIO

B etty Luceigh, PhD, has spent her life integrating her profession in organic chemistry with her reflections on the meaning of human experience. Dr. Luceigh earned her BS at the University of California, Berkeley (Chemistry, 1966), and her PhD at Stanford University (Organic Chemistry, 1970). She contributed to the chemistry profession predominantly through teaching her award-winning lectures in organic chemistry, the last eighteen years at UCLA (Senior Lecturer). Her creative activities in chemical education included the publication of some of the first computer-animated instructional CDs in organic chemistry (CHEM TV).

Dr. Luceigh continued privately to write poetry and short essays about her reflections on life as she wrote detailed public chemistry lectures. Her lifelong search has been to understand the relationship between science and spirit. She earned a Bachelor of Natural Theology in Sacred Healing (1989) at the Healing Light Center Church Seminary and was ordained a Minister of Healing. Since retiring to the country in 2004, Dr. Luceigh has continued to write from her unique perspective of the process of unification with more emphasis on spirituality and our connection to Earth. Her poems and essays have been included in multiple publications, including *The Ecozoic Reader, The Fallen Leaf Anthology* (Stanford "Write Retreats") and *Sierra Wonders.* She published a collection of her poetry entitled *Posit Poems: A 50-Year Collection from an Inquisitive Heart* (2011). She also shares current writings on her website (http://www.positpoems.com). One of Dr. Luceigh's gifts is her visionary voice inviting greater understanding and compassion toward all.

Appendix B

INDEX OF POEMS

GUIDED VISUALIZATION AND TEACHING: *BEAUTY IN THE GREEN VALLEY*

*B*efore beginning, seat yourself comfortably. Breathe slowly and deeply in a regular rhythm. Focus on each inhalation and exhalation as you relax into this moment. As much as gently possible, set aside distracting thoughts. Enjoy visualizing in your mind's eye the described scene with you as a participant. When there is a "Pause," take as much time as you need to visualize the scene and allow the experience to arise within you. Read slowly and then close your eyes while pausing. If you become uncomfortable for any reason at any time, simply stop, attend to your discomfort, and return whenever you are ready to do so. (Options: prerecord what is written here or have someone read to you.)

* * *

Visualize yourself standing alone in a natural valley in the early morning. All around you are very high mountains with steep slopes. They are covered with fresh springtime vegetation.

Pause.

There are green trees on the mountainsides and scattered on the valley floor. Everywhere you look, there are tall, green, wild grasses waving in a gentle breeze. There are buds of wildflowers on green stalks preparing to blossom patches of their own colors.

Pause.

A narrow stream flows gently through the valley floor. It splashes over rocks and ripples over sand. It broadens into a small, clear lake with its surface mirroring the mountains. Fish occasionally jump as if simply for the joy of it—or perhaps to look at you, the only human ever to be in this place.

Pause.

In the sky between the mountaintops, there are scattered clouds brilliantly lit by the morning sun. Birds appear—some flying in search of food, others drinking at the river, others sitting on branches singing to no one in particular. Insects offer arrhythmic sounds to the background of the river's flow.

Pause.

Turn around slowly to observe everything surrounding you. It is all pristine nature. There is nothing and no one to threaten you in any way. There are no growls, no roars, no hisses, no yells, and no judgments. Continue to inhale and exhale with an inner feeling of serenity and safety.

Pause.

Walk by the river until you find a rock to sit upon. Let your mind release whatever thoughts have recently distracted you. Observe, simply observe, everything that surrounds you in *this* moment—not only mountains, stream, clouds, and birds, but also whatever else comes into view before you.

Pause.

Imagine that your eyes magically drift from your head down to your chest, just over your heart, to become "eyes of the heart." With those eyes, see thin ribbons of light connecting everything in the valley to everything else. See thin ribbons of light also connecting the valley to you. Let the light from the *valley* enter through your heart's eyes with each inhalation of breath; let the light of *you* release outward from your heart with each exhalation. In this way, you are in wordless communication with the valley, light *to* and light *from* each other.

Pause.

Rest in the peace of your experience as you read (or listen to) the teaching below.

Everything you sense in this valley, including you, can only be sensed in the moment of Now. Everything you sense coexists with everything else in the same moment. Everything you sense came forth from a unique combination of parts created within the Kosmos. Whether tree, stream, or bird, each has a history of its travels through time past; each has uncharted travel in time yet to come.

But at *this* moment, another moment of Now, everything

is simply *being* what it is within this moment. Everything in this valley *is* of the Whole of the valley. You, as human, not only bear witness with human awareness but also experience your *own* human existence, your *own being,* within that of all existence connected to and communicating with *you.*

This is an experience of the essence of Beauty: *wordless Unification by conscious connection to everything in the present moment.*

Beauty exists within everything as a common quality. She is the *unifying* force within all existence, offering mergence to those humans who would drop the pretense of isolation. It is a pretense not found in trees and clouds and birds and fish. In their presence, such as in the green valley, they give us humans encouragement to *be* as we are in each moment.

Beauty flows between human hearts in order that each may have the experience within itself of liberation through authentic connection, of expansion through sacred origins of being, and of appreciation of diverse combinations of creation. Beauty is our shared legacy, giving rise to our shared longings.

At any time, wherever you are, you can return to this green valley of Beauty if you call upon the presence of Beauty within your own heart.

* * *

Continue to quietly inhale and exhale with eyes closed until you move out of the visualization of the green valley and into your present surroundings. Give gratitude for any lessons you may have experienced. Know that this green valley awaits your presence at any time.

Roses Unfolding

Forever and ever!

Printed in the United States
By Bookmasters